SALT BOX

An Old-time Yankee Looks at Modern America

by
Phil Dudley

Illustrated by
Paige Miglio

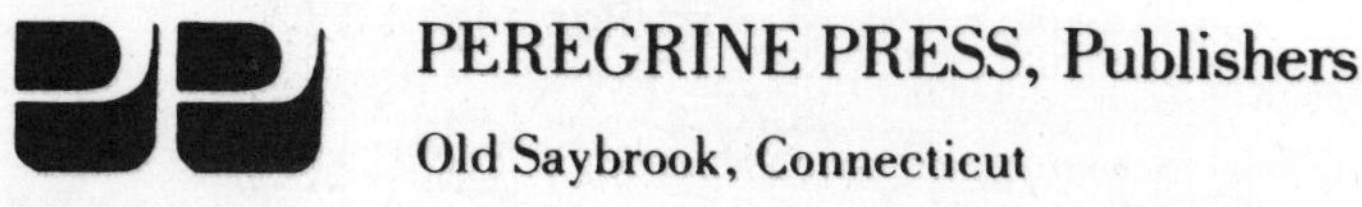

PEREGRINE PRESS, Publishers

Old Saybrook, Connecticut

Copyright © 1982 by Phil Dudley. All rights reserved. No portion of this book may be reproduced in any form without written permission of the publisher, except by a reviewer who may quote brief passages in a review.

Most of the commentaries in this book appeared originally in slightly different form in the column *Salt Box* published in the *Shoreline Times*, Guilford, Connecticut.

Cover design by Marie-Louise

Book design by Hildebrandt Associates

Illustrated by Paige Miglio

Cover photo by Ann Logan

Manufactured in the United States of America

First Printing

ISBN 0-933614-18-7

Table of Contents

A Pinch of Salt — An Introduction

Staid ways of old New England and fleeting philosophies of the atomic age; firmly programmed Yankees and infinitely flexible computers — such are the contrasting phenomena of my lifetime.

I like to delve into them, for I'm a part of them. Old-timers glean wisps of yesterday from the fields of today, and young folks find the past brand new. So here is a collection of the thoughts of an old-time Yankee as he observes American life in the latter part of the twentieth century.

It's named Salt Box. Perhaps, like salt, it can add to the flavor of other peoples' cogitations. Besides, I feel at ease with this homely reminder of the old kitchen container, and I live among the New England houses whose sensible shape has made Salt Box their name.

Some may choose to savor this book a little at a time, measured like the "pinch of salt" in an old recipe. Hence, although the subjects lie loosely around a seasonal frame, they are strewn at random for the piquancy of suspense.

— Phil Dudley

I'm A Fugitive!

Old year? New year? What about it? Review the past twelvemonth? Guess what will happen in the next? Do all those things? Don't do any of 'em?

For me, last year was so good that, like the GI in one of Bill Mauldin's cartoons, I feel like a fugitive from the law of averages.

The Law of Averages is defined as "a statistical principle formulated by Jacques Bronouilli to show a more or less predictable ratio between the number of random trials of an event and its occurrence.

Now let's not get side-tracked trying to find a more or less predictable ratio between "more predictable" and "less predictable." Just let Jacques' thing be a law unto itself!

I'm mulling over some occurrences of events that generally happen every now and then, but in the random trials of last year, didn't turn up at all — or at least not as often as I'd expect. From that viewpoint, I'm scared to death of next year.

For instance, my ''random trials'' included two visits to the dentist. Even though an inordinate proportion of my enamel, dentin and pulp has been superseded by gold and baser metals, there's enough left to produce cavities. But there weren't any. Hence the law of averages leaves me down-in-the-mouth about the probability of drilling next year.

It's been a long time since I've had a flat tire on the road. Some day I'll be ticketed by the law of averages on that.

Random trials on the adherence of four-year-old paint to the clapboards of my house indicate that I'll be wielding a brush next year.

My check book has balanced at first trial ten times out of the last twelve monthly statements. That's too good a record to hold through another year.

We had very few crackin' thunder showers last summer. My wife is deathly afraid of 'em, so the law of averages is right on her heels.

Last summer was so dry I didn't have to rev up the lawn mower at all for a six-week stretch. Can that happen two summers in a row?

Of course the law of averages requires that every law have at least one loophole. In my case, this has to do with fish bones. If there's one anywhere in the fillet it will surely turn up in my helping. Yet the last time I had to have a doctor fish a fish bone out of my mouth was in 1927 — and I'll bet the law applies next year.

Last year I set out for some twenty concerts or theater performances without ever leaving the tickets at home. Wow!

I fell asleep while reading in bed and left the light

on for half the night only 238 times. This could happen 365 nights.

Never last year did my Peugeot run out of gas on the highway.

I found someone else's mail in my post office box only 17 times during the year.

Someone has laughed at my corny jokes more than 88 per cent of the times I've sprung them — even the third or fourth time.

Only once has anyone at a cocktail party jostled my elbow so I spilled my drink on the hostess's rug.

Last year has been too good to me. Statistics are closing in. Predictable ratios presage disaster for next year.

More, more than less, I try to evade the law of averages, but that light is flashing in the rear view mirror. I'm a fugitive. I must pull over and face the odds.

According to the law of averages, though, things seldom turn out to be as bad as you expect them to be. Happy New Year!

Inkwells and Pigtails

''Still sits the school house by the road, a ragged beggar sunning,'' wrote Whittier. Just so sits the Clapboard Hill School, last of its kind in Guilford, and so it sat even in its livelier times. Blue weed tall in the yard awaited the late-August visit of a neighbor with a scythe, preparing for fall opening.

That yard would have to be 20 times as large to meet today's minimum acreage formula for an elementary school. It was compact but busy. There was room for Haley-Over, a game of tossing a ball over the school house to a team on the other side. Hide-and-Seek was feasible around the school, the big elm tree and the honeysuckle-blanketed stone wall. The yard would do for Cut-Across or even baseball.

In snow, we'd tramp out a huge cart-wheel pattern for Fox-and-Geese, or build a fort to be stormed by snowball-hurling troops. A stone wall was modified to form a hut, and down the road a cave was dug into the bank and roofed with old boards. A swing hung from an elm branch seemed like the world's highest. All this, with minor excursions into a physiology textbook, constituted physical education, rarely structured, never dull.

A small auxiliary building discreetly partitioned into two sections, each with strong up-draft ventilation, took care of sanitation.

A pail of water on a shelf in the entry, with community dipper, constituted drinking fountain and wash room. A pupil delegation drew water daily from the well at a neighboring house. Eventually the pail and dipper were retired in favor of a spigot-equipped tank and paper cups.

School bus? Never heard of it. Transportation was by shoes or bikes. For lucky me, if the snow was packed, a quick run and bellyflop onto the Flexible Flyer could jet me from our back door to the school steps — or down the hill a half-mile to East Creek, an attractive alternative!

Inside the building? A dozen double desks and benches, a teacher's desk, a wood-burning stove, and blackboard-lined walls.

Also, one teacher and up to two dozen youngsters of assorted sizes and dispositions, distributed through eight grades. Is there a unionized 1980's school-marm who would undertake lesson preparation and scheduling for such a program?

The school superintendent dropped in occasionally to see how things were going. Another sometime visitor was the truant officer whose game leg with six-inch-thick shoe sole lent extra ominousness to his august presence.

Whispering was taboo, giggling was frowned upon, passing notes was clandestine, and you didn't dip the pigtails of the girl in front of you into the ink-well on your desk unless you really loved her and needed to get her attention.

We came out well-schooled. Grammar, sentence structure, spelling and multiplication tables were drilled into us. We read ''Heidi,'' memorized ''Sheridan's Ride,'' and knew the heroes of US history. A third-or-fourth-grader could augment his courses by eavesdropping on the recitations of the upper grades.

Admittedly some glaring weaknesses occurred. The teacher who was there in my second-grade year shook my confidence by teaching us that the St. Lawrence River flowed from the Atlantic Ocean into the Great Lakes. It had to. That was its downward slant on the wall map that was pulled down over the blackboard!

Still — all too still — sits that school house, harboring memories of people long before my day, as well as mine.

What Kind of Weather?

''This is no kind of weather to have diarrhea in!''

That edifying line popped out at me from a commercial on television Sunday night. On the TV screen, it was raining, and this chap was arriving at home in the downpour.

As for me, I'd been home for quite a while, afflicted with a totally different complaint — a cold complete with sniffles and sneezes. Outside, the weather was cold and blustery, and the thermometer hadn't gone above 20 all day. Is that any kind of weather to have a cold in?

(Incidentally, is ''in'' any kind of preposition to end a sentence with?)

If that's the kind of weather to have a cold in, chalk up some brownie points for me. I did it right. The Dudley theory, however, puts it the other way around. A cold is the kind of thing to have such weather in. Oh, sure, it comes from a virus no one has learned to combat; but it happens more often in February than in August.

On a bright February morning about 60 years ago I felt logy, and went out for fresh air. In boots and jacket I sloshed through the slush in the pasture, finding rabbit tracks and other items of interest to a country boy. Then I stopped at my cousins' house to tell them about the hike. Next day I had measles. The sunshine hadn't helped me, nor my cousins who shortly came down with the measles also. Was that any kind of weather to have measles in?

My grandfather's "rheumatiz" used to kick up when a wet spell was in the offing. He was a better forecaster than the professionals. There must be a kind of weather not to have rheumatism in.

John Burroughs voiced "a chronic anxiety about the weather," but George Gissing took another view: "For a man sound in body and serene in mind there is no such thing as bad weather." It's easy to go on from there to the conclusion that for the purpose of having diarrhea, any kind of weather will do.

Then speaks more introspective Robert Frost: "Your head so much concerned with outer, mine with inner weather."

Inner weather may spring from outer. Often I welcome a rainy day; it's relaxing, and my spirits rise. That may be a throwback from farming days. Endowed with antipathy for labor, I'd find in a rainy day some respite, conscience-free, from heavy outdoor work. We might go to the corn house and shell a few bushels, then pick up the cobs and clean the place, chasing mice for sport. A harness strap might be mended, or a book read. There is a kind of weather to take a breather in.

Who needs what weather? The farmer wants a

steady all-night rain to perk up his wilting crops one week; and a four-day dry spell so he can harvest hay the next. The man with the maple grove needs cool nights and warm days to bring the flow of sap to his buckets. The market gardener hopes frost will not nip his tender plants in spring, but wants a November freeze to put flavor in the turnips before he pulls them. There's a kind of weather to do each sort of work in.

Snow sends the ski buff to the slopes. Zero nights make the pond safe for the youngsters' skating. The summer sailor looks for blue sky and a stiff breeze. There's a kind of weather for each enthusiast to play in.

The Book of Ecclesiastes sets forth a time for nearly everything. Similarly, perhaps there's a kind of weather for everything. But that TV commercial poses a puzzler. How do I get to the bottom of the matter? Write to the pharmaceutical house that was doing the advertising? To the agency that produced the commercial? To my family physician? It's urgent for me to find out exactly what kind of weather to have diarrhea in!

Reflections

My mirror in the morning brings little cheer. I see a wide-open yawn, centered in a stretch of stubble that'll have to be mowed down. Better I reflect on other mirrors.

Take the one in the front hall, for example. It's not only a different mirror, but I once approached it with a different eye. It's round, with no frame. One day we framed it with Christmas garlands to take a photo for the family greeting card. We posed on the stairs and my brother aimed the camera at our image in the mirror. Then came the question — should he focus for the distance from camera to mirror, or from camera to mirror to subject? Sharp and erudite discussion didn't resolve the matter, but the one-minute-print camera did. The combined distance was correct. We came out sharp and clear while the greens around the mirror were softly out of focus for a lovely picture. The camera's lens is not as tolerant as the human eye.

The mirror in the car is small, but geared to gather information — how close is the chap back there who is tailgating, and is he moving into the passing lane?

A mirror just like that was mounted on the music rack of the organ console in First Church sanctuary. In it I, as organist, could see when the ushers were through receiving the offering, and in it I saw the expectancy of many a bride as the doors opened for her to come up the aisle to the altar.

The mirror in my mouth makes it hard to answer the questions that the dentist keeps asking. I open wide and cogitate on the fact that I've never seen the backsides of my front teeth. I wonder, too, whether it's much of a problem for the dentist to work with the mirror image. I'd hate to have him nudge the drill in the wrong direction.

The full-length mirror in the men's furnishings store has three panels. There I see myself from angles I don't ordinarily catch, and find some points I'd never noticed before. The jacket almost fits. This image is much less depressing than the one with which I started the day.

Then we go to a restaurant, get seated and place our order. Looking around, we suddenly see ourselves over there across the room. The whole wall is a mirror. The place is only half as big as it seems.

A mirror can fool you in many ways. Two Guilford fire companies responded to an alarm one night when fire had broken out in a Mulberry Point cottage. Each took a hose line in from a different side of the building and the fire was quickly doused. When they began to mop up, they discovered that one of the lines had indeed put out the fire. The other had hosed down a mirror in another room where the blaze was reflected.

The mirror's deceptiveness is turned to profit in amusement parks where people pay to see themselves looking fat or skinny, tall or squat, straight or twisted. The relentless honesty of the mirror, on the other hand, is marshaled in markets to help combat human deception. Through its convex eye the shoplifter may be spotted.

A lake is an inspiring mirror, doubling the loveliness of mountains or fall foliage in glassy smoothness or in rippled softness. Another time, a shimmering path of moonlight may lie along that miraculous mirror.

Into the mirror of humanity the politician gazes, groping for reflections of attitude and opinion which may threaten him, or on which he may ride to prominence and power.

Most intimate, though, is the mirror of the individual. Each person gives off a reflection all his own, and in return I tend to respond in the spirit in which I'm greeted.

As George Herbert wrote two-and-a-half centuries ago, "The best mirror is an old friend."

Cold Comfort

Sheltered is how I feel this morning. The thermometer outside sits at nine below zero. Here I am, all cozy under the electric blanket in a room where the temperature is 58. I awaken to all that comfort without having lifted a finger to achieve it.

That gives pause, and pausing, I read the Law of Inverse Appreciation: "The less there is between you and the environment, the more you appreciate the environment."

Between me and the environment right now is an elaborate structure, insulated and with storm sash. It also contains appurtenances to counteract the absence of heat in the outside environment. These, of course, are dependent on power flowing in through three wires from lines at the street, but they have neverthe-less shown great reliability.

The environment used to be closer to me, and its impact more direct. This bred a healthy respect for it — appreciation or not.

I'd wake up warm and cozy, yes, wearing an outing flannel nightshirt and tucked under layers of quilts. But the environment had invaded the room, for it was then considered healthful to sleep with the window open. I couldn't see the thermometer, but if there was ice in the earthenware container underneath the bed, I knew the weather was frigid outdoors. The thing to do was grab some clothes and scamper downstairs to the living room where the red-hot round belly of the coal stove gave off a flood of warmth. We never heard of the "degree days" which now tell the oil man when he'll have to get to us. We just knew when the coal bin in the cellar was getting low, and how fast the woodpile that fed the kitchen range was being used up.

Our "plumbing" was outdoors. There, as no-where else, one could achieve intimate contact with the environment — to such an extent that purposeful-ness flourished and accomplishment was achieved with all the dispatch one could muster.

Saturday nights brought another encounter with the environment, for then youngsters had to take baths whether they felt they needed them or not. We'd bring in a galvanized iron washtub from the bench on the back porch — so cold that a wet hand would freeze onto it. Set it in front of the open door of the oven with the fire in the kitchen range well stoked, pour in a big teakettlefull of boiling water and enough cold to make it habitable, and sit down in the tub.

Outside, one little morning brush with the environment was to dump out the solid ice from the water pan in the hen house and fill the container so the chickens might drink before it froze again. In the barn, though, the acrid heat of the horse stables and the mellower fragrance that steamed up where the cows were stanchioned gave welcome comfort for the chore-doer.

"Wind chill factor" is another modern invention we hadn't heard about. We simply knew that when the mercury was near the bottom of the tube and the wind was howling out of the northwest you could freeze your ears in no time at all.

So here I am, sheltered to a degree that draws a tinge of uneasiness from recollections of lesser shelter and from a vestigial remnant of Puritanical ethic — it can't be right to be so comfortable.

Bear With Me

Most recent among my bear acquaintances is Paddington, who was present at a recent family dinner. He wasn't at the table, but came downstairs for after-dinner conversation, of which he promptly became the center.

Paddington is about two feet tall. I first met him on Christmas Day, when he was unwrapped with unabashed joy, not by a child, but by a relative only a few years short of my own ripe old age. She hugged and kissed him, and now takes him to bed with her every

night and starts each day with endearments addressed to him. Otherwise this lady is mature and rational.

Bears seem to have something special. Ungainly and often unfriendly in real life, they are adaptable and durable as symbols and playthings. My relative who owns Paddington has made many sets of little dolls representing Goldilocks and the three bears.

Many other animals, of course, are dear to the hearts of youngsters. Snoopy, the dog in *Peanuts*, is a favorite of my grandson. Mickey Mouse with Minnie and the rest of his entourage has marked his 50th birthday. My best-liked non-bear is Pogo the possum, whose recent demise is an American tragedy.

Paddington with his charm and aplomb is immortalized in a series of books by Michael Bond. Like the other characters I've mentioned, he is being commercialized in media ranging from miniatures to T-shirts.

Then there's Teddy. Who would ever expect the name of Theodore Roosevelt, big game hunter, Rough Rider of San Juan Hill, President of the United States, to be attached to a cuddly little brown animal doll loved by millions of children?

Teddy Bear dates back to 1902, when President Roosevelt refused to shoot a captured bear cub while on a hunting trip, and the incident was subject of a newspaper cartoon. A Brooklyn store owner, Morris Michton, had his wife make a few stuffed bears, sent one to the President, got permission to use the name, and so was born a $150-million-a-year toy business.

Says John Noble, toy curator of the Museum of the City of New York, "Teddy's utterly trustworthy, honest. He's the perfect confidant. You can tell him anything and you know it's safe." This goes for Paddington, too.

Among the bears I've known, Winnie-the-Pooh rates high. A.A. Milne endowed him with whimsical and utterly disarming logic. Younger than Teddy but older than Paddington, Pooh is an off-beat bear who appeals to me.

I would not ignore the great propaganda bear, Smokey, who wears the hat of a forest ranger and preaches about preventing forest fires. He's one of the most successful gimmicks ever devised for promoting protection of natural resources.

This brings me to Yellowstone Park, where a traffic tie-up doesn't mean an accident up ahead, but usually one or more bears being fed by imprudent tourists. I came upon such a scene in Banff National Park where a bear and three cubs were getting attention. The mother bear reared up and pawed one foolhardy woman, but quit when she found what she had scented — a paper bag of sandwiches. I snapped a picture of the incident and forthwith retired to a previously prepared position — inside my car.

For a time around 1930 my home town harbored a real live bear, kept on a tether chain in front of a residence on Route US 1. One day I, the milkman, trotted up the driveway with the daily delivery and heard a shout, ''Get back in your truck! The bear is loose!'' I did. The lady of the house came out, quietly approached the animal and fastened his chain.

Incidentally, the traffic direction sign at a nearby fork in the road had no bearing on the customary presence of this peculiar pet, even though it read BEAR LEFT FOR GUILFORD.

My acquaintance with Paddington has triggered a rambling line of reference and reminiscence. I trust it hasn't been unbearable.

New Dirty Words

What is happening to the good old English language? I've found it always effective and often beautiful. I hate to see it mutilated.

Of course it changes with usage. Through the centuries such change has been gradual, usually in response to a need for easier, though not always clearer, expression.

Now, however, comes a forced change, crammed down our throats by a militant faction. A new ''dirty word'' emerges — simply three letters, m-a-n. The contention is that it's got to go, being sexist and unfair to the female sector of the race. This is the hottest witch hunt since the days when Senator Joe McCarthy was envisioning a Communist behind every bush, so I must be exceedingly careful.

I believe the language will suffer immeasurably from the persondate that the wopersons' rights activists have issued. Even the proud US Navy has run up the white flag and scuttled the title designating Annapolis students. Hereafter they'll be "midshippersons."

If I were a girl, should I be ashamed that Oliver Wendell Holmes in his classic defense of Old Ironsides wrote, "Ay, tear *her* tattered ensign down," and again, "Nail to the mast *her* holy flag . . . and give *her* to the god of storms"?

Preservation of the language may call for a committee. A strong chairperson could doubtless personage to set up a study of the personifold aspects of the problem. The matter could be approached from persony, persony angles. It is not a personufactured issue.

Sawdust in My Eye

Sawdust is in the public eye — serving as fuel in the huge Pinchbeck greenhouses in Guilford, to take the place of oil.

I first found sawdust more than 70 years ago. Then, a tiny finger probing and perhaps stretching the rip in a seam in Teddy Bear's cloth skin would bring some of that fascinating stuff out of the bear's innards. I could find it packed loose in the rag doll, too; or stuffed tight in Grandma's pincushion.

Sawdust in the Teddy Bear was coarse and scratchy. Out in the shop beside the vise on my uncle's workbench I could find some that was fine and silky-soft.

Years later, sawdust really got in my eyes, swirling away from the screaming saw at the winter woodpile. We felled trees in the farm woodlot, cut them into eight-or-ten-foot lengths and carted them home. When the woodpile got to be ten or twenty cords, we'd have Sam Blatchley come in with his saw rig. He'd wind up the big single-cylinder engine, and its make-and-break governor brought spellbinding suspense with long lapses between irregular stretches of rhythmic firing. But the big flywheels kept whirling. The saw clipped small sticks and ground grimly through bigger logs. Stove-length wood piled up for splitting, and a heap of sawdust rose beneath the saw table, around Sam's boots.

The sawdust was taken to the barn for bedding in the box stalls where Arline and Petey, our horses, lived. The stables needed much more bedding than the woodpile produced, though; and we got it, naturally, from the crayon shop!

A small factory in the next town turned out Alpha Dustless crayon for use on school blackboards. This was packed in wooden boxes and shipped in crates, so the establishment had a woodworking shop where whitewood was planed and cut to size for the boxes. Shavings and sawdust were blown through an overhead wooden duct to a small shed.

Now and then my Dad and I would gather up a pile of empty feed bags and go to the ''chalk shop'' for bedding. I held the bags while he shoveled it in — except for what the wind blew into my eyes. We'd tie the bags shut, pile them onto the wagon, bind the load with a rope and bring it home.

In those pre-Frigidaire days Steve Roberts, the Bishop boys and the Wilcox brothers watched their thermometers in the winter, waiting for their ponds to freeze a foot thick. Then they'd start cutting ice, and bring the huge blocks to the ice houses for storage. To keep the ice from melting before the hot months when it would be hacked into refrigerator-size chunks for sale, they packed it — that's right — in sawdust! It was a good insulator.

Sawdust smells good. Each wood has its own special aroma, always pleasant. That, along with its absorbency, qualified it for use on the floor in the meat market — and in the saloon, too, I'm told. I was not encouraged to go there.

Nor did I happen to take the "sawdust trail" — the sinner's road to rehabilitation, named from the sawdust-covered aisles in tents that housed revival meetings.

Sometimes I wonder if our society will be forgiven for one of its most flagrant sins — wastefulness. From a hotel window in Prince George, British Columbia, I saw the eternal flame at the top of a tall stack. Methane gas, by-product of a lumber mill, was being burned off. Throughout that area fat semiconical silo-like structures belched smoke and heat as sawdust was fired just to get it out of the way.

So it warms the cockles of my heart to see the gentle plume of smoke over Bill Pinchbeck's greenhouses where heat from sawdust keeps the roses warm. Conservation may be its fancy name, but to me it's just a good old Yankee try at putting some waste to work.

Pursuit of Happiness

Emblazoned in bold type across the newspaper pages I see messages reflecting the quality of America's respect and appreciation for two of the greatest Presidents.

The snows of Valley Forge melt into insignificance. The siege of Yorktown stretches into years beyond recall. The portrait of George Washington graces full-page advertisements proclaiming release from tyranny in the 1980's.

Tyranny? Yes, the oppression which that five-year-old car imposes upon us with its balding tires, tired battery, battered fenders. In the name of the Father of Our Country we may be delivered from the burden of pouring high-priced gasoline into an outdated guzzler.

Page after page promises rebates to those who buy new cars. Therein lies apparent relief from the taxation without representation laid upon us by potentates of industry through their customary, non-Presidents Day, ordinary prices.

On another page the prestige of the first President is invoked through the magic of his birthday sale to enlist us in the forces that can relieve a merchant of his burdensome overstock of overcoats and suits, allegedly to our great benefit.

Augmenting freedom comes emancipation—an unshackling from the slavery of cooking and the drudgery of housecleaning. This is under the aegis of Abraham Lincoln, whose portrait heads advertisements for self-cleaning ovens, self-defrosting refrigerators, super vacuum cleaners, all geared to the pace of this century's living.

This advertising is of course reliable. There is the picture of the beloved President who said, ''It is true that you may fool all of the people some of the time; you can even fool some of the people all of the time; but you can't fool all of the people all of the time.''

Now comes the crowning accomplishment — clearing the way for the pursuit of happiness. Neither President Washington, guiding the newborn republic through its perilous formative years, nor President Lincoln, burdened by the agonies of war to preserve that nation's unity, could have foreseen this twentieth century triumph.

I doubt that they expected their birthdays to be set aside as national holidays. Even less would they have imagined that those birth dates would become movable, to be shuttled back and forth across the calendar's checkerboard so that long weekends could be created.

In 1982 comes a masterful move in that game. Lincoln's Birthday, February 12, falls on a Friday, automatically stretching a weekend. Washington's Birthday, February 22, comes on a Monday, the day of the week to which holidays are so often being shunted. Yet this fortunate coincidence is not enough; Washington's Birthday is being jumped ahead a full week to Monday, February 15, to team up with Lincoln's for a four-day weekend.

Since they were men of liberal outlook and political savvy, I'm sure the father of the country would have no objection to joining with America's discoverer, Christopher Columbus; and the great emancipator would approve of enlisting Robert E. Lee, beloved leader of the defeated armies of the South, together with Martin Luther King, martyred prophet of fuller emancipation, for a spectacular linking of their five birthdays, Monday through Friday, resulting in a glorious nine-day weekend.

What skiing! What cruises! What sales! How the inspiration engendered by the memory of the two greatest Presidents would accelerate the flow of the currency that carries their portraits!

Can this be the America they built? Is this commercializing of their names and memories worthy of them or of us? Said George Washington: ''Labor to keep alive in your breast that little spark of celestial fire — conscience.''

To Rule the Roast

''Now wouldn't you like to rule the roast . . . '' sang Melissa in *Princess Ida*.

Rule the roast? I always thought it was rule the roost.'' That's how we usually hear it, and that's the way it is in the dictionary. So I read the footnote in my *Treasury of Gilbert and Sullivan*:

''The modern accepted version, 'rule the roost,' is a corruption of the original expression. To 'rule the roast' is to be in supreme charge of an ox roasting on a spit.''

I think we should go back to the original. More people would relate to it. Very few now-a-days can instantly visualize the poultry roost, nor its ruler, whether that be the hen who has worked to the top of the pecking order or the rooster with the most bravado.

But the roast! The suburbanite dons his fancy apron with a wisecrack emblazoned upon it, puts on the chef's hat, and sallies forth to bring the charcoal in the hibachi to exactly the right glow under its thin mask of white ash. Woe unto anyone who presumes to tell him when to turn the shish kebab, or hint that it has cooked long enough. He is in supreme charge of the meat on the spit, and is insanely jealous of that position. He rules the roast.

The same chap on a winter night lays the kindling and the logs in the fireplace to an exact position, lights the fire and resents any wiseacre who thinks he knows a better way to add logs or to juggle them into place. Figuratively, he rules the roast. That expression, dating from the sixteenth century, is only one of many to have suffered corruption through careless usage.

Time and again we hear someone assert righteously, "Money is the root of all evil." Even the most pious and fastidious cannot thoughtfully rally to the support of that statement, for they know that money can be an instrument of good.

Paul in his letter to Timothy (I Tim. 10:6) said no such thing. His words, intact through a multitude of translations, are: "The *love* of money is the root of all evil." This is a different concept, even though too all-encompassing to be fully defensible.

Another common mis-quote that doesn't give the author's full import is "blood, sweat and tears." When Winston Churchill took on the awesome responsibility of being England's wartime Prime Minister, the precise prescription he offered to his countrymen was "blood, toil, tears and sweat."

Occasionally someone will sagely observe, "A little knowledge is a dangerous thing." That does reflect the gist of Alexander Pope's verse, but without the gracious lilt of the original:

"A little *learning* is a dangerous thing:
Drink deep, or taste not the Pierian spring;

There shallow draughts intoxicate the brain,
And drinking largely sobers us again.''

Having taken the book down from the shelf and opened it to Pope's *An Essay on Criticism*, I treated myself to another draught, and found my free-wheeling fault-finding brought down a peg:

''Whoever thinks a faultless piece to see,
Thinks what ne'er was, nor is, nor e'er shall be.
In every work regard the writer's end . . .
And if the same be just, the conduct true,
Applause, in spite of trivial faults, is due.''

Spring Thaw

I haven't seen a robin on the lawn, nor heard peepers in the frog pond. March 21 is still two weeks away. Yet I know it is spring. I get the message when I drive out of the driveway and jounce into a hole in the pavement.

Pot holes make news. They cause disgruntled taxpayers to call Town Hall. Not much use to patch them, though, until the road dries out and ''settles.'' Most people demand smooth surface right away, but this old-timer hates to see tax money dumped into a hole only to be squished out by the first truck that comes along. Wouldn't spring be tough on politicians if it came at election time!

Picture the pre-hard-top times! On this same road, any low-slung car just sits on its belly and spins its wheels in the mud. The Model T Ford can usually make it, being high off the ground and having a two-pedal-no-clutch gear shift great for rocking the car forward and back. Even better is the horse and buggy, with mud dripping from the spokes as the high wheels in their slow turning bring it up.

There's Dr. Milo Rindge, out to make house calls come mud or high water, walking to get help when his car is mired.

For an eight-year-old, slogging in spring mud is fun. Sink in deep, but not over the top of the rubber boots — and hear the lovely slur-r-r-r-schlop as the boot comes up, slowly, so the suction doesn't pull it off. A mud dam in the gutter makes a pond for sailing boats whittled from pieces of shingle. Dig a ditch from rut to rut, then to the gutter, and see the water trickle down the lively little river.

Finally, March winds dry out the ground. Then comes the grader drawn by a four-horse team, slowly, for the blade now and then hits a boulder. Dirt, sod, cobblestones are drawn toward the center, making a high-crowned road with gutters to drain it. Then the drag smooths it.

On the hills they make thank-you-ma'ams — dams across the road to divert rain water. This device gets its name, I'm told, because the wagon jouncing over it produces what looks like a courtly bow on the part of the driver.

Ecology? Never heard of it! Yet this old highway drainage system is superb for keeping water on the land, for it has no pavement, catch basins or culverts.

Even now, though, in the age of pavement and potholes, the sun and wind work their magic. Problems evaporate. Patience is the key.

Cookie Sheet

A carload of cookies? It seems so. The Girl Scouts with their simple, resistance-proof sales pitch have taken orders. Now come the crunch — so to speak. The shipment arrives and deliveries must be made.

Leaders, mothers, Scouts proceed with enthusiasm edging toward desperation, and with inefficiency unequalled in the annals of merchandising. Pennies roll into the coffers of Scouting and dollars into the dividends of manufacturers. Housewives' resolutions to shop price-consciously and to quit nibbling sweets melt away. Everyone is happy.

Puzzlement, disappointment, amazement and occasional satisfaction can be derived from the shelves of the supermarket, too. Big cookies, little ones, sugared sandwiches, plain wafers, filled cookies are there. Some are savory, others taste like sweetened sawdust.

To me, though, those aren't cookies at all. I had three grandmothers who made ginger cookies. I liked the cookies and loved the grandmothers, and the cookies were as different as the grandmothers were.

My own mother's mother made them big and thick and moist, almost square. They were not crisp, but I knew I had my teeth into something when I munched one of those molasses-loaded treats.

My step-mother's mother made ginger cookies thin, crisp and light-colored, with spicy tang. I could eat one after another until the jar was empty, and still be ready for more.

The ginger cookies I grew up with during my first six years, in the home of my father's mother, were round and quite thick, just moderately crisp especially when fresh from the oven.

None of those recipes do I have. There is in my jar one named ''Snacktime Molasses Cookie.'' To make it, sift together a cup-and-a-half of sifted flour, three-fourths of a teaspoonful of baking soda and a half-teaspoon of salt. Then cream a half-cup of shortening and three-fourths cup of sugar, and blend in one egg and one-fourth cup of molasses. Sift the dry ingredients into that and mix 'em up. Add a half-cup of moist coconut and a half-cup of chopped walnuts. Then drop the dough by level tablespoonfuls, about two inches apart on a greased cookie sheet. Bake at 375 degrees for eight or ten minutes, and cool only slightly before taking them off the sheet. They're good.

My wife also turns out chocolate chip cookies and a little ginger-spice one that ''tastes like more'' but makes me thirsty. I hope the three grandchildren who now head for the cookie jar at our house may find there the makings of memories as precious as those I cherish from threescore years ago.

Hymns Misplaced

Commentary on the fitness of things was made by my uncle, Edmund F. Dudley, as he sat on the porch at his Indian Cove cottage on Sunday evening watching the faithful file through the bevy of bathers to gather for vespers on the point of rocks beyond the beach.

''I don't believe in singing hymns at the beach,'' he mused, ''nor diving in church.''

Sleepers and Sinners

''The normal American Sunday, having been crammed full of things there isn't time for during the working week, has become the most highly pressured day of the week,'' writes Alan Olmstead in his book, *Threshold*. He goes on to mention breakfast, the Sunday papers, some open-air project for which only week-ends offer enough time, and the nap without which Sunday would not be Sunday.

The busy Sunday did not exist in the Guilford of my early years. The livestock were fed and the cow was milked, and beyond that no work was allowed other than getting the meals.

On Sunday morning we'd hear the bells of the four churches around the Green — First Congregational, Third Congregational, Christ Episcopal, and Methodist — ringing in measured sequence. They pealed at 10:30 and tolled at 10:40, calling people to the 10:45 services.

Sunday ritual I remember from earliest childhood was going out under the apple tree in the yard with my father, to have an orange—not an everyday treat! Later, it was having a grapefruit at my grandmother's house. Since my mother died when I was born, I lived first in my grandparents' household. When I was six, my father remarried. I loaded my toys into my express wagon and trundled it across the field to our new home. Years later I learned that my uncle lured me to my grandmother's with grapefruit each Sunday because I was so contented in my new home that I seldom ran over to visit my grandmother, and she missed me.

The Dudleys went to church on Sundays. The day of a blizzard in the 1920's my father, two uncles and I were almost the whole congregation.

Families always sat in the same pews, for the seats were rented — a church support system later supplanted by the every-member canvass. Letting the ladies alight from the buggies at the carriage step in front of the church, the men folks would drive around to the sheds behind the church to tie up their teams. There they would discuss the world, the town, their crops, their families. The Doxology was sung at the beginning of the service, and they felt that if they came in when they heard that, it was soon enough.

Unless the sermon was long, church was out at noon. Then came Sunday School with classes for all who would stay, from tots to graybeards.

So dinner was late, but that didn't matter. The rest of the day had to be devoted to not doing anything a youngster would like to do. We could read or go for a walk, but never play ball or build a bird house.

And oh, the nap that Alan mentioned! My grandfather, my father, my uncles, even my grandmother would drop off to sleep and snore the afternoon away. I didn't see how anyone could sleep in the daytime, but now I understand it better!

Came the automobile. At first we'd sit and watch the "sinners' parade" of Sunday motorists go by. Little by little, we began to join them. Even before the automobile, the Cornell family would get the surrey out for a Sunday drive. This elicited the comment by pious Mr. Nelson Dudley, after lightning had struck the Cornell barn, "I should think more barns would be burned — so much ridin' on Sunday."

Still, we didn't work. New-mown hay should lie untouched on Sunday even when rain was threatened for Monday.

I'm not typical. For more than 50 years my Sunday mornings have been filled with work—playing the organ for church services. Beyond this, though, I have changed along with the rest. Some 20 years ago I painted my house in spare time, but never touched a brush on Sunday. Today I'm likely to paint, mow the lawn, or tackle almost any other chore that needs to be done on Sunday.

If longtime First Selectman Leslie I. Dudley reads this, I can imagine his slow grin and sardonic chuckle. He will remember the 1938 hurricane, after which his public works crew was stretched flat out opening tree-blocked streets. Reinforcements came when a WPA gang from East Haven arrived to clean up the Green where 90 huge elms had been uprooted. They began on a Sunday morning. I wrote a "letter to the editor" deploring this unseemly disturbance of Sabbath quiet. After the paper came out, Les commented: "I wish I could play the organ. I'd go up there and underbid that guy."

Amazing Maze

I've just staggered out into the open from that amazing maze — the wonderful world of Form 1040. It was an intriguing adventure, scampering along one passageway after another in the network built by the Internal Revenue Service.

"Subtract line 40 from line 39. Enter here and on Form 1040, line 33. (If line 40 is more than line 39, see the instructions for line 41 on page 18.)"

Then I try, "Subtract line 3 from line 2. If line 3 is more than line 2, enter zero."

Backing out of that little cul-de-sac, I head down a long corridor, through the file of checkbook stubs and receipted bills, evidence of medical expenses, listing trips to doctors in New Haven at some-odd cents a mile; finding balance of insurance premiums not listed on line 1; sorting the expenses into categories; adding lines 4 through 6c.

Now turn a corner. Back to the first page and punch the pocket computer to find three per cent of line 31. Enter it on line 8. Subtract line 8 from line 7. If line 8 is more than line 7, enter zero. That tortuous trek leads only to a big, fat, ever-lovin' zero. No deduction at all. A blind alley.

Oh-oh! Here it says, "You must report embezzled or other illegal income." Very well. I'll list that. But wait! "We may give the information to the Department of Justice and to other Federal agencies, as provided by law. We may also give it to the States, the District of Columbia . . . to carry out their tax laws." Best forget those items.

''Dividends are distributions of money, stock or other property that corporations pay to stockholders.'' Well, well! Learn something every day.

''You can deduct gambling losses, but not more than the gambling winnings you reported on Form 1040, line 21.'' Uncle Sam is not gambling!

Here's a column headed, ''IRS Will Figure Your Tax and Some of Your Credits.'' *Some* of my credits? I think I'll figure it myself.

This is a bargain: ''If you were married on December 31, consider yourself married for the whole year.'' But you must not deduct the fee for the marriage license, nor for driver's, dog or hunting licenses.

I dare you to try this one: ''These instructions apply only if there is an entry on Form 4952, Investment Interest Expense Deduction, line 22 and Schedule D, lines 20 and 21 (or Form 4798, lines 8 and 9) and both show a gain.''

Then taking the smallest of three figures derived from other forms, ''Enter this amount in the margin to the right of Schedule D, line 20 (or Form 4798, Part I, line 8). Identify by writing next to it: 'From Form 4952.' Subtract the ordinary income from the gains on Schedule D, lines 20 and 21 (or Form 4798, Part I, lines 8 and 9). In addition enter the ordinary gain on Form 4797, Supplemental Schedule of Gains and Losses, Part II, line 10. If you do not use Form 4797 for other transactions, enter it on Form 1040, line 15, and identify it in the margin as 'From Form 4952.' ''

I'm glad I didn't take that one. I'm tired, though, from darting this way and that through one line after another, doubling around to get out of dead-ends, trying to guess the right turns. Finally I burst into the clear, through line 54 — but only to reach for the check book.

What manner of maze is this, where the *correct* route gives you the shock? Misguided mice we are!

New Songs for Old

I sense in the bird populace a long-term shift, bringing cardinals and mockingbirds to this region where a few years ago they were seldom seen. Oppossums, too, now scurry across our roads, glaring at us with their ugly little pointed visages. They, too, were formerly deemed denizens of the South.

We used to have a wren house on the clothesline pole, with entrance hole the size of the quarter so that larger birds couldn't squeeze in. Jenny Wren and her husband came each spring, bubbling with song and lugging in twigs for their nest. In summer they found juicy bugs in the pea vines of the garden, and dashed tirelessly to and fro bringing these morsels to their tiny family.

On another pole was a bluebird house, larger and deeper with entrance near the top. These lovely birds provided velvet-toned alto in the morning chorus.

Noisy martins lived in their multi-roomed house next door. We could set the calendar by them in the spring. First came a few scouts, then the whole flock, to spend the summer chasing flying insects and dive-bombing the dog.

Barn swallows cemented their nests in the torrid reaches of rafters high above the hay mow, but skimmed at low altitude where the mosquitoes were.

Sometimes they'd perch in long rows on the telephone wires preening their feathers — a portent of rain.

Another masonry nest was that of the phoebes over the porch. These flycatchers threw an aggressive throaty note into the morning song ensemble.

The bob-o-link swung on a tall stalk of mullein, pouring his torrent of song over the hay field where his mate sat on their hidden nest; and the meadowlark from his favorite perch on a high pole sent a clear call above all the others.

Those birds may be somewhere, but they do not come to our neighborhood the way they used to. House finches, starlings and sparrows are always with us, and soon we'll hear the spring symphony, curtailed though it be. The liquid notes of the red-winged blackbirds already issue from the marshes.

A few days ago I picked up from the porch floor the stiff little body of a female cardinal who had mistaken our breezeway for a throughway. Next morning from the tip-top of the maple tree Mr. Cardinal in gorgeous red was sending out his call of challenge, triumph, passion, joy. That morning, though, I just couldn't hear it that way.

Patience

My grandmother was a quiet woman of considerable forbearance. One day, exasperated by some impetuosity of my grandfather, she said firmly, "You must have a tremendous lot of patience, Francis. I've never seen you use any of it!"

The Dump Age

Diapers aren't laundered, flashlight batteries aren't renewed, razors don't get new blades. Everything is chucked into the rubbish as soon as it's used. This is the "disposable age," with planned obsolescence built into appliances and automobiles.

When I was a milkman, part of the delivery job was to pick up the empties. The glass bottles were washed, sterilized and used time after time. Now the milk comes in a plastic jug, non-biodegradable, which eventually helps to fill the town dump.

During World War I we children collected tinfoil for some aspect of the war effort. It might take a month to get together a ball the size of the wad of foil the average householder today throws out. In World War II, Guilford's First Selectman invented a lifter to wrench abandoned trolley track rails out of the street pavements for scrap iron. But now, abandoned cars are a blot on the landscape and a glut in the scrap market.

Some states have enacted "bottle bills" to encourage recycling, cut down on solid waste and reduce roadside litter. Guilford has addressed the problem in another way, organizing Guilford Recycling, Inc., to reap profits through sale of glass, aluminum and paper.

Kooks who delight in smashing bottles on the streets should be sentenced to serve time feeding the glassbreaking machine at the recycling center. There they could revel in a deafening, soul-satisfying symphony of shattering glass — no pipsqueak clink of one breaking bottle, but a wholesale shower of shards.

I'd like to be here a thousand years from now, watching the archaeologists try to reconstruct the civilization of our age on the basis of their finds in systematic "digs" on our disposal sites.

Ceramics, plastics might be there, some imprinted with a mysterious awkward system of material communication. Coils of copper wire, some substantial, others tiny, might survive — their use a mystery. Tests might reveal extensive traces of oxidized metal, the only residue of our transportation. Evidence would be not of an age of atom or computer, but of dump.

No Curtain Call

In the lexicon of my life, *curtain* has come to be synonomous with *exasperation*. The term, of course, includes window shades and draperies. Although these shield us from glaring light and prying eyes, they are nevertheless loaded with potential for mischief and aggravation.

My heart is still pounding from the fright the window shade — another form of curtain — just gave me. Out of dead silence burst the crash of the shade zooming from sill level to top roll when its little catch let go. It set my teeth on edge and my hair on end.

Spring wound too tight? I'll fix it. Release the roller from its bracket at the business end and unroll the shade part way. Now try it. It stops languidly at half-mast. When I take it off again, the spring unwinds in a finger-numbing spasm. Zero is then the starting point in the search for the elusive balance between limp futility and sinister tension.

Again, on a summer night, the window is open and the shade partly lowered. There's not a breath of air, but finally I get to sleep. That shade, though, is merely biding its time. Just before dawn a little breeze springs up. Flap . . . flap . . . flap, gently, annoyingly goes the shade. When I can't stand it any longer, I get up and raise it. Light from the sunrise floods the room, and I'm too stirred up to sleep any more.

Drapes, another breed of curtain, can team up with a breeze to give me a hard time. The wind is brisk and I'm closing a window on the leeward side of the house. The drapes sail outward. I draw the left-hand one in, but the closing window pinches the other. The job requires three hands, but like the average householder, I have only two.

The innate perversity of drapes comes out when I'm hanging them. Working each hook into place lifts out the one I've just hooked in. Then when I get to the end of the row, there's one left over. Somewhere along the line, craning my neck to aim the tri-focals, I skipped one. Start all over again, but don't give up. As Fielding wrote, "Nothing more aggravates ill success than the near approach to good."

Hanging the shower curtain offers the same problem coupled with the adventure of standing in the bathtub and stretching to struggle with those pesky eyelets reluctant to be nudged into the plastic rings.

In that curtain, too, lurks damaging deviltry. Warily it waits for morning, when I come in there half asleep, aware only that I must hurry. I juggle hot and cold spigots, capture and recapture the soap, finish showering and step out into a puddle of water on the bathroom floor. That perverse curtain was hanging outside the edge of the tub — not inside where it belonged.

Years ago, side curtains were an accessory of the good old Model T Ford. Their oblong eyelets fitted onto twisty fasteners along the top and down the sides. I've been drenched while putting them on under a sudden summer shower, and froze my fingers while fastening them one frigid winter morning. Once installed, those curtains would fend off about ninety per cent of the rain, or sixty per cent of the cold wind, while their yellowing plastic windows cut visibility to about fifteen per cent.

Even the theater curtain has its perverse drawbacks, so to speak. It keeps me waiting expectantly until just seventeen seconds before the hefty foursome of latecomers edges into the row with heels crucifying my corns and coatsleeves mussing my hair. What was that bit of business onstage that has the audience in stitches? I'll never know.

I shouldn't get so testy over my inept struggles with curtains, though. Wrote George M. Cohan, "Hurried and worried until we're buried, and there's no curtain call; life's a very funny proposition after all."

Things I Need

"What in the world is that?"

"It's a riveter. Uses split rivets or tubular ones, to fasten harness straps. Or belts."

"It's rusty and you don't need it. Let's throw it out."

"No. It works perfectly well and it might come in handy sometime."

"All right. But certainly you don't want all this old pipe."

"Maybe not. But if I hadn't had some of it lying around, that railing I built for the cellar stairs last winter would have cost plenty."

"What do you have there?"

"A rifle."

"A rifle? How do you shoot anything with that?"

"You don't. You sharpen your scythe. Hold the scythe so the blade points away from you and slap each side of it with this double-faced carborundum stick."

"Oh. But for heaven's sake don't keep anything you don't need. This cellar is a mess, and you always have to keep everything."

So I threw out whatever I didn't need. A fellow does need a good many things, though.

Take this old baby carriage, for instance. I'll move these window screens so you can see it, when I take the cartons of berry baskets out of it. The high iron wheels were made before rubber tires came along. It used to have a parasol held up by a clamp bracket, but that's long gone. When I was a baby I rode in it. Years later, it's a wonder my little brother survived, the way I would run full tilt down the sandy road with him in the carriage squealing with glee. It hasn't been used lately, and most likely won't be. But I need it.

No, this isn't a wrench. It's a tool for prying drive-in calks out of horseshoes. The sharp calks kept the horse from slipping on the ice. When they wore down, you'd have to pry them loose and hammer in new ones. Better keep it around.

And that harness punch. That'll go with the riveter. You can make new holes in a leather belt, as you lose weight.

Here's an iron stake to drive in the ground, with a swivel and chain on it, to tether out the calf so she can mow the lawn.

Look at these huge hinges! Sure, they're rusty. They held the doors on that shed that stood out in front of here before we built the house — the shed we tore down and put the lumber in the attic to build an extra room sometime, but never got around to that and used it for the garage instead. Boy, what hinges!

This milk pail with shield and strainer was almost a musical instrument. Tzing, tzang, ting, twang it went when the alternate streams from the cow's udder hit its shiny bottom. Then the frothy white fluid rose in the pail to muffle the sound. Kind of need that.

Here's a cardboard keg labeled Dari-Rich Chocolate Syrup. It held 50 pounds of luscious goo which Hill Crest Dairy mixed with milk the likes of which you can't buy now, to make a summer drink with substance to it. I used to distribute it on the daily milk route. That keg with its round wooden bottom makes a great waste basket for the cellar. Make sure it doesn't go to the dump.

Oh, ho! An eight-quart milk bottle carrier. I've lugged that to many a door stoop, delivering full bottles and picking up the empties. It was handy, too, for fending off the family dog if he didn't like the milkman. It's good to have now, because there's nothing more exasperating than trying to keep cans and jars from tipping over and rolling all around in the car.

Well, well! A flashlight on a headband, with battery case to clip to your belt, great for a skunk-hunting trip on an October night. Put in some batteries and I bet it'll still work.

Now here's a super plumb-bob. String right out of the middle of the top and silvery cone with sharp point at the bottom. It was with surveyor's instruments belonging to my great-uncle who was a civil engineer. Have to keep that.

That's how it goes, cleaning the cellar. I took a load to the dump, but most things I stowed away again because I need them.

Memorial Memories

Memories lived within the old house, behind weathered clapboards and tiny window panes, sheathed in heavy fragrance of the untended lilacs that enveloped the place more closely every year. There we came, each Memorial Day, to glean from them some garlands for the cemetery.

Other blossoms, mostly those of pink wild honeysuckle, had been gathered from the roadside during the six-mile ride from home, as my mother and her mother returned to their family homestead for the day. There was room for the flowers in the two-seated wagon, and time to pick them as the horse threaded his way through Podunk's narrow-cut road and labored up Flat Rock Hill.

Then we went to the cemetery. While the family graves were being tended and decorated, I ranged over the lot, placing flowers on every grave that bore a flag or a marker indicating that a veteran was sheltered there. The hills, the forest, the farms stretching north and west seemed to be just as they must have looked in the time of the Civil War. Some gravestones bore dates far earlier than that.

Through my young mind coursed such school-boy-memorized lines as Finch's:

"Under the sod and the dew,
Waiting the judgment day,
Under the laurel the Blue,
Under the willow the Gray."

This family-oriented celebration of Memorial Day drew me away from the ceremonies that took place in Guilford which was our real home town. My young friends took part in them, gathering flowers from fields and gardens and carrying them in the parade to set them lovingly on the graves of veterans. This personalized ritual, however, has been discontinued. Now flags and potted geraniums are placed by the veteran's organizations prior to the services.

Neverthless Memorial Day clings to the spirit and the purpose of the Decoration Day established by General John Logan so long ago. Veterans and Scouts, with flags flying proudly in the spring sunshine, step to martial tunes of school bands. The stirring music yields to a hush as the parade enters the cemetery, moving to the rim-shot rhythm of a single drum. Prayers are said. Volleys crack and echo. *Taps* floats over flowers and graves, to be echoed from a distant corner. Can the throat stay clear, the sight un-dimmed?

And then, turning from the formality of this ceremony, I hear from behind the oppressive curtain of holiday traffic noise, across a half-century of time, drifting from that lilac-mantled house and distant rural burying ground, General Logan's admonition: "Let no vandalism or avarice or neglect, no ravages of time, testify to present or coming generations that we have forgotten, as a people, the cost of a free and un-divided republic."

No Suckers There

A nineteenth century town meeting in Guilford dealt with the offer by a well-to-do citizen to donate the pipe for a seven-mile water main from Lake Quonnipaug to the Center, provided the town would install it. The voters in less than infinite wisdom rejected the proposal. The discussion, however, seemed interminable. One objection was that a costly pumping station might be required.

At this point canny Deacon John W. Norton observed, "If some of these people could suck as hard as they can blow, we wouldn't need any pumping station."

Where Goes Only?

Let's look at some of the horrible things that happen every day to our beautiful, baffling English language — and pray that neither the author's carelessness nor the type-scrambling gremlin will create any special instances.

We'll only see a few examples — oops! There's one now! I mean, we'll see only a few examples. What's the difference? The first one says either that we're not going to do anything at all except see a few examples, or else that we're not going to do anything with the examples except see them. The "only" has to follow the "see" in order to say what I mean — that the examples we see will be limited to just a few.

"I miss not having the car, now that George uses it every day," complains Mary. She misses *not* having the car? No, no. Mary's trying to tell us that she misses *having* the car.

"It's so inconvenient for George and I," she goes on. Of course she'd say "It's so inconvenient for me" if that were the full sentence. But when George gets in between, Mary fails to carry the sense of the preposition past his name.

"All right, all right," she explodes. If anyone wants to hear about my problems, they'll have to take my grammar the way it comes."

Now, Mary dear, you've stepped into a quagmire where you'll find plenty of company. A dozen years ago I could have told you simply that the two pronouns ought to be in the same singular number — "If anyone wants . . . he will have to . . . ." The pronoun "he" was acceptably used in genderless context to mean "he or she." But now the super-sensitive women's lib element imposes awkward revisions in the language. Your best bet is to foil 'em with a different construction: "Anyone who wants to hear about my problems will have to take my grammar the way it comes."

Let's be fair to Mary, though. Her school probably didn't put its pupils through the sentence-parsing drills that used to be applied. Furthermore, on television and radio, on the street and from the podium she hears all sorts of linguistic atrocities.

Even Presidents trip up. Eisenhower used to say "nucular." That one's continually seeping out of the reactors, polluting the air beyond my tolerance level. The word is "nuclear." Noo-klee-ar, not noo-kew-ler.

Some words get an extra syllable thrown in — ath-a-letic for athletic, trans-a-lation for translation, and Real-i-tor for Realtor, for example.

Am I nit-picking? You haven't seen anything yet! Here's the ultimate. When I picked up my prescription at the drug store, neatly typed on the label were the words, "Take one capsule four times a day." That poor capsule will be in bad shape before bedtime. Taking it four times a day is impossible, yet no more difficult than finding any other concise way to phrase the directions. That one has me stymied.

Then there's the pomposity of officialese. One day a Guilford police cruiser was dispatched to an accident near a specified intersection of streets. The officer in the squad car radioed for more precise directions. Came the response from the desk officer: "As you approach the area, you will be able to determine the exact location by visual observation." (Translation: "You'll see it when you get there.")

Mary's still here, apologizing because she arrived late. "George couldn't back the car out because the dog was laying in the driveway," she says.

A hen with her eggs, possibly; but not the dog. He was *lying* there. So now I'll lay down my cudgel and let it lie right where I laid it yesterday, on the spot where it has always lain.

Numbers, Please!

"Getting high-hat, aren't you! Don't you even wave to a friend when you meet him?"

Family and friends have tossed that kind of remark at me for years. Often I cannot identify a person through his windshield in time to wave when our cars are meeting at ordinary speeds.

Recently I began to astonish them. They'd even comment about it. "He actually waved to me on Boston Street this morning!"

The secret? I set out to learn license plate numbers. As my repertoire grew, I became more and more socially acceptable, recognizing friends and waving gaily.

Then without warning came the calamity. With minimal fanfare and little notice of hearings, the Connecticut General Assembly ordered the discontinuance of the front markers. Fertile though the Assembly is in the field of doubtful wisdom, you'd have to pore through the annals very thoroughly to find a more stupid piece of legislation.

I'm not implying that front license plates should be required simply to keep me in the good graces of my acquaintances. They are for a more serious purpose, of course — identification by the police or by a witness. Now isn't two-way identification twice as good as one-way?

Economy is the stated reason for the legislation. To put an obstacle in the way of law enforcement? To have citizens drive miles for the purpose of returning number plates? If ever there were a nit-picking piece of false economy, here it is.

I'd rather economize by eliminating slogans from license plates. "Constitution State," "Vacation Land," "Sunshine State," "Land o' Lakes," or what have you, mess up the marker. Clutter cuts down clarity. Furthermore, I question the state's right to make my car an advertising billboard.

Getting back to those bare bumpers, I wonder what lobby bought that bill through the Assembly — speeders, robbers or a coalition?

It used to be, "They'll get you going or coming." Now it's only "going."

Turn Down the Wick

The Rochester kerosene lamp — cylindrical wick, glass chimney, green chinaware shade — stands on the table in the living room of a Guilford farm home. The time is about 8:30 in the evening; the year, 1918. A three-months-old baby snuggles in his basket, making the uncouth little noises babies do while they sleep. The housewife is in the kitchen.

Elbows on the table, head in his two hands, book open flat under the lamplight, sits a ten-year-old boy, engrossed in the saga of Tom Swift and his motorboat. He is annoyed by little black specks that keep settling on the pages, but he blows them away and keeps on reading.

The mother, sensing something amiss, comes in from the kitchen to find the lamp smoking, its chimney black, the air heavy with flaky soot, the tablecloth flecked with the pesky precipitation. She turns down the wick, whisks the baby's basket to the kitchen. The boy brushes soot flakes out of his hair while absorbing a lecture about anyone who can get so wrapped up in a book that he doesn't know what's going on right there beside his head.

Surely there's no idea in his head that 64 years later he'll see in that evening's predicament a parallel to one of the major problems of a later era.

Now he's in 1982. The universal wick is creeping up. The air is loaded with pollution both visible and invisible — particulates from industrial processes, combustion, forest fires, dust. Even worse are totally unseen elements — toxic carbon monoxide, lung-irritating nitrogen oxides, cough-breeding photochemical oxidants, and oxides of sulfur. These come from motor vehicle engines, industrial boilers, electric generating plants, industries using solvents, and those burning sulfur-containing coal and oil.

The populace, although sometimes annoyed by evidence of such pollution, is generally oblivious to it. Head in hands, figuratively, it goes on reading and working and fretting, unaware that the pollution causes or aggravates respiratory ailments, colds, emphysema, heart disease, eye irritations and cancer. Pollution costs the public billions of dollars a year through damage to health, property and vegetation.

Mother could open the windows and air out the room. She could scrub the paint, sweep the floor, launder the tablecloth. But when the atmosphere — that blanket around the earth which supports plant and animal and human life — is polluted, cleaning it is practically impossible.

Even more to the point, mother could turn down the lamp wick, stopping the trouble at its source. What prevents such action today on a world-wide scale? Concentration does — not merely engrossment in other matters making the public oblivious to the hazards, but rather a deliberate and total concentration on immediate profit; on production regardless of ultimate cost.

A materialistically-oriented administration in Washington, supported by and kowtowing to corporate America, is nullifying protective regulations representing years of dedicated effort. The nation needs a government willing to curb this pursuit of the fast buck, and able to turn down the wick.

Genius of Medley

The mockingbird sings from the tip of my tall spruce tree. He woke me before five this morning. He may be she, or perhaps they take turns. They look alike — big as a robin but more slender and longer-tailed, gray above and white below with white patches on wings and tail, conspicuous in flight.

Last year I complained when a crow took up the habit of perching in the tree outside my window at sunrise, calling raucously to distant cronies. The mockingbird is different. The crow had a one-track mind, but the mockingbird switches off in many directions.

If he keeps me awake, it's to wonder what's coming next. It may be a carol rich as the robin's or the oriole's or sweet as the song of the house finch. He can do the click of the grackle, or cut the air with a replica of the blue jay's alarm. The throaty ''phree-bee'' of the phoebe comes easily to him, but he may shift glibly into the thin clear ''fee-bee'' that's the chickadee's call; or he can give a tiny trill like the tree toad's.

Yes, he's a mimic; but also an original and ingenious improviser. He may be picking up and echoing tunes too faint and far away for me to hear, but I'm sure he's also composing on his own. He can devise variations on a theme — even on a theme I whistle to him.

According to my bird guide, his song is ''an indescribable medley, sometimes very sweet and pleasing; at others, harsh and unmusical.'' I nominate him for the versatility award.

Whatever he does, he repeats it a few times before launching into the next episode. The book says that the brown thrasher usually repeats once; and the catbird, not at all. But the mockingbird will do it over and over. He has even the savants doing it, too. The scientific name for his Eastern variety is "mimus polyglottos polyglottos." Polyglot, of course, means "a mixture or confusion of language."

The bird that awoke me at dawn was still singing three hours later. At noon he was warbling on in the treetop. In late afternoon he bubbled over with melody. At twilight he regaled me with vesper varieties. The throat that can forge those silver tones must be ironclad. Even Pavarotti couldn't match this non-stop vocalizing. The mockingbird merits a medal for stamina and tenacity.

Yet he can be quiet. I set my tape recorder in the window to capture his rapture for winter enjoyment. Silence ensued. The tape rolled on but the microphone had nothing to transmit. Did the mockingbird know? Was some special ESP telling him I was about to infringe on his copyright?

My old bird guide (1906) describes the mockingbird's range as "Southern U.S., breeding north to New Jersey (and casually farther)." I resent the insinuation in those parentheses. My mockingbird is not breeding "casually." He's utterly respectable, so jealous and protective of his home and family that I can't even find them. Some years ago he set up housekeeping in my lilac bush, but I didn't discover it until after his family had grown up and left. That year he sang from my rooftop. Now he's at the apex of the spruce, proud but not at all casual.

I hope his appetite is for Gypsy Moth caterpillars. World Book says the mockingbird eats insects, weed seeds and wild fruits, and has modernized his food habits to such an extent that he's been seen picking insects off the radiators of parked cars. My mockingbird sings so incessantly he must find little time to forage for food. In appreciation, I should snare some bugs in the grille of my Peugeot and set it out there to serve as his automat.

Lawn Vs. Garden

Suburbia breeds two kinds of people — lawn people and garden people. They are incompatible.

Garden people dig up sections of lawn so they can plant flowers. Lawn people then have to mow around and trim close to the flower beds. Garden people till their soil diligently, picking out pebbles and storing them in little piles hidden in the adjoining grass. Lawn people then have to resharpen their blades.

The garden person at my house, plagued by rabbits nibbling off the tender tulip shoots, heard tell that empty bottles laid out in the garden with the wind whistling across their tops would keep the bunnies away. Bottles were duly placed. The tulips had their season. June, July and August came and went. The flower bed was neglected and weeds flourished. In September the lawn person sought and received permission to mow them down. There was music with unprintable lyrics when the rotary mower hit the hidden glassware!

Lawn people have trials and tribulations, beginning with establishing a lawn. We tackled ours after a long winter of balancing on board walks across the mud flats around the new house. It was 1937. Prosperity was not rampant. First Selectman Les Dudley gladly granted two-day leave of absence without pay to a couple of the best men in the public works crew so I could hire them for the final raking and seeding.

The grass sprouted, first sparse and then thick and green and thirsty. You can't water a quarter-acre lawn from a deep well rated two gallons a minute and supplying two households and a dairy barn. So you rig a jerry-built system with an old pump precariously hung in an abandoned shallow well. It works. You can ignore the skeptical comments of relatives and neighbors.

Next come plantain, sorrel, blue weed, dock, Indian paint brush, daisies, buttercups, thistles and three varieties of dandelion. You dig 'em up, smother 'em with healthy grass, jab 'em with poison-squirting wand, sprinkle 'em with weed-killing fertilizer. They prosper. Finally you notice that they are a reasonable facsimile of grass. You relax and leave them be.

Whatever the vegetation, it grows and grows and has to be cut, unless a merciful August drought slows it down.

My uncle fenced his lawn and turned in a couple of sheep. They did a fine job of close cropping, and added special fertilizer that brought in a stand of white clover.

My dad would set the crowbar and tether chain to pasture a cow on the lawn. The grass was kept short, but with a tendency to develop small patches where it was taller and greener!

After sweating it out for a year or two with a hand-pushed reel mower, this lawn person acquired a big old used Moto-Mower. Magneto long gone, it drew ignition current from dry cells in a box bolted onto one side. The engine was borrowed to run the water pump on the dairy farm the day the 1938 hurricane knocked out electric power. That mower was a sound investment, bought for $35, used for eight years, sold for $35.

The next two trials were errors. A little rotary was inadequate and its recalcitrant two-cycle engine sapped my patience. A kooky hand-pushed device cutting grass with interlocking gear-like discs was useless on my tufty turf.

Fascinating was the Snappin' Turtle which could be tethered to a stake so it would run in a widening spiral. This was impractical on two counts. The lawn was not circular, and the sight of this machine chugging over the lawn all by itself was a traffic hazard as drivers stopped to gawk. Used with conventional personal guidance, however, it was the best mower this lawn person ever had.

The later luxury of a riding mower was abandoned as the lawn's rough terrain joggled my innards into disarray. Now I walk behind a **power**-propelled rotary, good exercise and more productive than jogging.

Still, the grass looks greener in the yards of the neighboring lawn people.

Ave Quisquiliae

Along a country road one day I noticed an abundance of specimens which apparently had never been subjected to formal analysis or orderly listing — an astounding miscellany ready for examination and collection by serious students, or by born pack-rats.

Responding to the challenge, I now touch the subject just enough to show that a fertile and neglected field lies open for research. I aim for scholarly description and classification to guide the beginning collector.

Flora (vegetation) and *fauna* (animals) of course have been studied thoroughly. I focus attention on *quisquiliae* (rubbish).

It is logical to start with the genus *cadus vitreous* (common name "bottle"). One common species falls into the sub-classification *fuscus*, basically cylindrical in body, tapering to a narrower mouth. It may measure from 20 to 30 centimeters in diameter, hollow with a shell in brown or amber version of the substance commonly termed "glass."

Another variety of this genus is *crystallus*, similar in many respects to *fuscus* but transparent and colorless. It is likely to be flattened in form, and may emit the odor of alcohol. Often a vari-colored label is present.

Cadus vitreous is frequently found in shattered condition. The shards have cutting edges and points exceedingly dangerous to the hands of collectors. Since their favorite habitat is roadsides, they also present a hazard for the pneumatic tires used on present-day vehicles.

Even more common is the genus *olla* in innumerable variations. *Olla stanna* (vulgarly known as tin can) is cylindrical with discs closing each end, in dimensions usually smaller than *cadus*. It is highly susceptible to the oxidation ordinarily known as rust. *Olla aluminia* closely resembles *stanna* but is deceptively light in weight, and is resistant to rust.

Specimens in both these classes are easily distorted or compressed. They are conspicuous in colorful markings, and many often be detected at considerable distance by the incidence of light rays reflected from their mirrorlike surfaces.

A radically different family of *quisquiliae* is *charta*, closely related to ancient Egyptian papyrus. Conspicuous in roadside habitat because of its size and abundance is *charta diurna*. This appears in large white sheets often grouped together, densely covered with black patterns ranging from two millimeters to eight centimeters in height, believed to be significant as a means of communication among individuals of *homo sapiens*.

Another is *charta academica*, a smaller single sheet characterized by symbols in varying degrees of refinement, usually literary or mathematical, often with red or blue notations such as "C-plus."

Chartae are subject to yellowing by long exposure to sunlight. They are fragile when waterlogged, but in dry condition are highly mobile and may be airborne for considerable distances, making their range wider than that of other *quisquiliae* of greater specific gravity. They are also readily flammable.

Numerous are hybrids between *ollae* and *chartae* — cellular specimens incredibly diverse in size, shape, structure and pliability. Some bear markings believed to indicate the nature of their original visceral mass. While many are only a few centimeters in length, I have seen one measuring nearly a meter, so engorged with smaller specimens of *quisquilae* that its skin had ruptured and it was disgorging them at random.

Quisquiliae are spawned in industrial, commercial and recreational centers of the North American continent and can tolerate nearly any environment. They are disseminated casually by some individuals of the animal species *homo sapiens* having little regard for the well being of other members of that species.

A diligent and serious collector, equipped with gloves, plastic bag or other convenient container, and commercial motor vehicle, can find surprises in new varieties continually uncovered, and satisfaction in the volume of specimens brought in.

Move We Adjourn

Guilford's Deacon Charles D. Hubbard hastened the adjournment of an over-long committee meeting by standing up and saying, "It's time honest men were in bed and thieves were about their business. I'm going home."

Almost Hot Enough

"Hot enough for you?"

To that overworked greeting I'm likely to respond, "Well, almost."

To some people I'm an enigma on a steamy day, because if the weather can't be just right, I'm happier with it too hot than too cold. I suffer more when the mercury drops below zero than when it soars past 90. Nevertheless, there are exceptions.

For instance, the car has to be locked, with windows closed tight, when I leave it. There it sits on the simmering blacktop, sun beating down on it and into its windows. The interior becomes an oven. The seat sears my anatomy when I get in. I can't touch the rim of the steering wheel. I crank down the windows for a breath of air. It's "hot enough for me."

Occasionally I've had to rummage in an attic — my grandmother's, my parents' or my own — to find something on an August afternoon. I love the nostalgia-loaded smell of dry wood and paper and cloth, and it's strongest on a hot day. But the wasps swing past my ears in loose-hung flight from their nests in the rafters. Sweat rolls off my face and arms, spotting priceless old papers. It's "hot enough for me."

Hot was the labor of raking and heaping and spreading and loading hay in the sun-baked fields. Then when the load came home and was backed through the wide doorway onto the barn floor between the two mows, it had to be pitched off — first down and then up as the mows were filled. Finally ''up'' meant over the great beam into the gable. Cob-webs blanketed the roof boards, mud wasps' structures and the barn swallows' nest clung to the rafters. The heat of the summer sun beating down on the shingled roof was concentrated unmercifully.

Whether lifted by forkful after laborious forkful, or hoisted by horse power, the hay had to be stowed away. That was usually my assignment. What a relief, when the load was off, to scramble down the ladder for a quaff of lemonade! The loft was ''hot enough for me.''

I'm not immune to heat. I gravitate to the shade on a hot day. Going to the beach to lie in the sun and be broiled is not for me. If the lawn has to be cut I'll wait until the sun is low in the west.

Furthermore, I refuse to work myself into a lather complaining about the weather. Is it hot enough for me? Rarely. Most likely a cool ''almost.''

Cows' Automat

Almost magic is the automation we saw on a farm in Vermont. This establishment on the shore of Lake Champlain has 1,500 acres, and capacity for 200 milking Holsteins. The manager runs it with only five employees.

Not only do machines milk the cows, but they rinse and sterilize themselves automatically. Scrapers creep across the stable floors four times a day (cows learning to step over them as they come along), to take out the manure, which is pumped to a slurry tank with six-month capacity.

The cows are rated in four classes — those producing 50 pounds or more of milk per day; those running between 40 and 50 pounds; the laggards below 40 pounds; and the "dry" cows between production periods.

They get a total ration mixture. High producers have six pounds of 40 per cent protein grain, 20 pounds of high moisture shell corn, and 30 pounds of haylage each day. These proportions are varied for the several production classes.

The blue-ribbon girls, those shelling out more than 50 pounds a day, wear an electronic device that meters out a pre-determined bonus of grain — an extra pound for each two-and-a-half pounds of milk over 50.

This gadget, called a transponder, activates the feeder to deliver the grain. It is calibrated to dispense a pound a minute, and can be set to operate from three to 50 minutes per day. A cow in the 60-pound bracket, for instance, could get an extra pound of grain four times. She's free to decide for herself just when she wants it.

Says the manufacturer: "When used in conjunction with current milk production performance, the transponder can be used to challenge the cow to produce milk up to her potential.

I've always wondered what a cow is thinking about as she stands there placidly chewing her cud. On this farm she may be saying to herself, "I'm not giving down quite all the milk I could, and I would surely enjoy an extra snack. Better give it the old college try and earn a bonus."

Or perhaps she's an up-to-date girl: "For heaven's sake, just look at my figure! I wouldn't dare get on the scales. Got to cut down on seconds at the feeder, so there's no use knocking myself out making more milk."

Seriously, though, this program makes sense scientifically and economically. It puts the feed where it will be most productive, and doesn't stuff the low producers beyond a point of diminishing returns.

Philosophically this sets off a whole train of thought. The free enterprise system, left to itself, tends to compensate the diligent and the thrifty; but it isn't always left to itself. Humanitarian considerations intrude. Disadvantaged people must be helped. This inevitably funnels some of the resources into the least productive elements of the society. More and more our government sets the transponder on the basis of factors other than performance. Where will this shift in motivation lead?

Looking at the huge barns, silo, slurry tank, supermodern machinery, I saw hefty capital expenditure. To make such resources available, the economic transponder must be set to deliver compensation commensurate with the risks involved.

The herdsman on this farm is a girl, doing a big job with full responsibility. She and a girl helper put the milking machines onto 140 cows in a couple of hours, a smooth-running operation. Yet she took the unexpected in stride. Her wholesome grin grew even wider when she got an unexpected milk bath while repairing a sudden break in the pipe line.

A young bull wandering into the wrong alley backed meekly away when she trotted in, slapped his face and said, "Bad boy! Go on back there!" She's an agricultural college graduate, and the farm manager says she's an excellent herdsman.

Magic though the automation may seem, it still must be directed and sometimes overridden by human expertise.

Caws For Alarm

The night was dead-still and stifling — one of those when even our hilltop house didn't catch any moving air. Sleep was fitful until that blessed hour just before dawn when night's coolness finally creeps into the room.

Then that sound sleep was shattered. A crow in the maple tree fifteen feet from my open window took up conversation with his companions. Judging by the volume, his remarks were addressed to compatriots in the next town.

The crows of Clapboard Hill grow more friendly from generation to generation. They perch on poles in the garden, making raucous comments on the general situation. They walk across our lawn, right up to the house, boldly snatching bread scraps intended for smaller birds.

We used to think of the crow as an exceedingly wary individual, unapproachable and not given to hanging around near the house or farm buildings. Like the blue jay, he was an alarm sounder for the whole forest, announcing any intruder by wild cawing. The crows congregated in a rookery bordering the fields.

Crows had a passion for pulling up seed corn just as it sprouted. A scarecrow or a dead crow hung on a pole might or might not deter them. At planting time we'd dump the seed corn into a tub and stir tar or crow repellent into it. This didn't make the corn planter operate any more smoothly, but it cooled the crows' yen for planted kernels.

As a youngster, I heard of instances where a crow had been tamed as an intelligent pet. Assuming that such training should begin early in the bird's life, I located a crow's nest at an altitude to which I could climb, and brought home a fledgeling.

That wasn't all I brought home. The bird was promptly exiled and ticketed for treatment with the louse powder that was kept on the shelf in the hen house. Furthermore, I underwent more thorough scrubbing than a small boy ordinarily does. I don't remember what happened to my pet eventually, but he never grew up to roost on my shoulder, retrieve shiny objects or otherwise excite the envy of my peers.

Back to the hot morning. Rudely awakened, I lay there after the crow had departed, sorting out other bird songs. A house wren bubbled its happy trill, and a distant robin was cheerfully chirruping. A grackle startled me as he cleared his throat while flying past only inches from the window. English sparrows were insistent. A nuthatch and a yellow warbler foraged for tidbits in the maple. A squirrel scooted down one branch and up another.

The crow? Off in the cool woods nursing his voice for tomorrow's sunrise klaxon!

Contest Is Ova

My own special version of "The Egg and I" surfaced in conversation with a friend the other day, so I started to tell him all about it.

This dates back to the early 1940's when thousands of eggs were thrust into my daily consciousness with the expectation that something constructive would be hatched. I'm sure I never embodied the "miracle of silent radiation and patience" which E. B. White notes in his priceless description of a broody hen — "all eye and tail."

At that time seventeen of the agricultural colleges in the United States conducted egg-laying contests — annual marathons for selected pullets from leading poultry breeding farms. Thirteen birds constituted a standard "pen." A breeder might enter one or two pens in a single contest and could enroll entries in as many of the contests as he chose. Once there, the birds performed under unbiased, uniform professional feeding and management.

"How could anyone keep score?" asked my friend.

By trapnesting. Whenever a biddy felt motherhood coming on, she did the usual thing — hopped into one of the cozy nests provided for that purpose. But in the contest, something new had been added. A trapdoor flipped so she couldn't come out until someone realesed her. That didn't disturb her, though. She laid her egg.

On our farm, collecting the eggs tended to be a once-a-day chore; but in these contests, not so. Frequent rounds by attendants were required. Whenever he found an occupied nest, he'd quietly lift the hen out, read the number on her leg band, and chalk up the egg to the credit of her account. Then he'd let her go, and the nest would be ready for the next one.

The game had yet more numbers. Each egg was weighed. Average egg size was a significant factor. So was livability. A bird had to have stamina to hang in there dropping an egg nearly every day. Whenever one of them called it quits and died, it was not only a black mark on the record but also a handicap for that pen during the rest of the contest.

"But what did all that have to do with you?" prodded my friend.

I'm coming to that. You see, those hard-headed poultry breeders didn't go to the trouble of entering the contests just for sport, nor even to see for themselves how their birds compared with others. They aimed to set records for the world to know — especially their customers.

To tell the world by magazine advertising, catalogs and radio, they needed someone to compile the facts, write the copy, plan the publicity program. That's an advertising agency, and Guilford had an up-and-coming agency called Yankee Writing Service specializing in poultry accounts. I worked there, writing some copy and holding the title of Research Director.

That's when all those eggs hit my fan. We had to know the score not merely for our clients, but also for every pen in the seventeen contests. We kept a monthly up-dated index with a card for every contestant. Nobody else in the country had such complete information on the statistics of egg-laying contests.

Toward the end of each year, as they came down the last lap or entered the home stretch — however you'd express it — the suspense grew. One year our Oregon client set world records for production by individual bird and by official pen, with his White Leghorns. Another time one of the major trade papers scrambled its egg figures and we nailed them for poaching our client's position. We had the facts to support superlative statements about many breeders' biddies.

"Did you ever buy any?" asked my friend?

Yes, I did. From the excellent Rhode Island Red strain developed by one of our clients.

"Aha! A victim of your own propaganda!"

No Remorse

A neighbor of ours, after sounding off sharply in a town meeting, concluded his remarks with: "If I've said anything I'm sorry for, I'm glad of it!"

Alleged Assault

Leafing through an old issue of the East Podunk Evening Chronicle, I noticed an article under the by-line of Walford W. Widgen. In the paper's listing of its staff, Mr. Widgen's title was Police News Reporter. I was so impressed by his mastery of the style characteristic of that field of reporting that I share it here:

At a time as yet undetermined, a reputedly female juvenile said by apparent witnesses to be wearing what seemed to be a red parka apparently entered a purported path in an evidently wooded area. It was asserted that she was carrying what looked to be a basket that in all likelihood contained food, which authorities conjectured that she intended to take to her so-called grandmother.

According to the statement which she gave police subsequent to the reported incident, she was accosted by an·alleged wolf. Conversation ascribed to the pair indicated that the intended destination of said juvenile may have been discussed. At any rate, it is assumed that after taking leave of her the alleged wolf probably proceeded to that possibly disclosed location.

Supporting this assumption, said so-called grandmother when later questioned by police affirmed that an alleged wolf appeared at what she claimed to be her home, and upon professing to be said female juvenile, gained probable entrance by way of an ostensible doorway. Thereupon he allegedly attacked the so-called grandmother and seemed to disguise himself in clothing evidently hers.

Subsequently, it is believed, said reputedly female juvenile arrived at said so-called grandmother's supposed residence. Upon announcing her purported arrival, she claims to have received what she deemed to be an invitation by her so-called grandmother to enter.

Once inside, she said, she noticed the supposed bedroom in apparent disorder, and detected there a suspicious individual, later determined to have probably been the alleged wolf, then alias so-called grandmother.

To her inquiry as to the size of his supposed eyes, he is reported to have replied, ''The better to see you with, my dear.''

Questioned about the seeming dimensions of his apparent ears, he said, according to the juvenile's statement, ''The better to hear you with, my dear.''

The statement further asserts that when the size of his evident teeth was mentioned, said alleged wolf responded, ''The better to eat you with, my dear,'' and thereupon set upon said juvenile purportedly intending to devour her.

At this point a group judged to be woodsmen apparently arrived, armed with implements believed to have been axes. Conflicting reports include the contention that the alleged wolf may have ingested one or both of the apparent victims. However, in view of the subsequent presence of the so-called grandmother and the reputedly female juvenile this hypothesis was discounted by police, who maintain that said supposed woodsmen inflicted possibly fatal injuries upon the perpetrator of the alleged attacks before he had opportunity to harm the apparent victims.

Pending an autopsy and further investigation, no charges have been lodged. Speculation, moreover, was that both said juvenile, tentatively identified as Red Riding Hood, and her so-called grandmother showed an easing of anxiety, indicating the probability that they would live happily throughout the foreseeable future.

The Dudley Heifer-Catcher

How to use a rat trap for catching a heifer is an item of useful information that may come in handy for any householder. Who can tell?

Most heifers are docile. You can catch one by walking toward her with quiet words and a handful of hay. She may even extend her head expecting you to give her the exquisite sensation of long scratching under her throat and chin.

When I was working on my uncle's dairy farm, one of the younger members of his herd developed an acute case of misanthrophy. Somehow she slipped through the pasture fence and thereafter would have nothing to do with people. Fleet-footed and crafty, she saw to it also that people might have nothing to do with her.

Pursuit was futile, strategy inadequate. She extended her range and reputation. Sightings were reported from various sections of town. One day we trailed her over a snowy mountain and down to the highway, but gave up after spotting her scampering like a mountain goat halfway up a sheer slope. Some time later she began to appear again in the vicinity of the home farm. At night she would enter the high-fenced yard off the bull's stable behind the barn to snatch some hay, since the gate was usually left open.

Now I'll tell you, as I promised, how to use a rat trap to catch a wild heifer.

Rig a rope and pulleys to a high post so it's capable of slamming the bull-pen gate shut.

Use a pail full of stones as a weight to power this rig.

Take one large snap-spring rat trap, drill a hole through its wooden base under the trigger and mount it vertically, high on the post.

Bring one end of a strong linen thread through the hole in the rat trap base and tie it to the trigger.

Spread some hay in the pen and stretch the thread from the trap across the hay, fastening the end to a fixed object on the opposite side of the pen.

Set the trap, with the pail of rocks suspended on the trigger wire.

Step over toward the hay and brush against the thread, testing the system to be sure the pail will be released and fall, yanking the rope to slam the gate shut.

Reset the the device and go home to supper and to bed.

Return next morning to greet the misanthropic bovine, trapped according to plan.

That's all. Mission accomplished, I enjoyed fringe benefits — semi-jealous joshing from the farm help, plaudits from the boss, fame of a front-page article in the home-town newspaper, entitled "Yankee Ingenuity Captures Heifer."

This simple heifer catcher can be set up by any rural resident. It is not patented. I have magnanimously made the plan available to the citizenry of this great nation. It demonstrates, like Phaedrus' fable of the Fox and the Raven, that ingenuity avails and wisdom is an overmatch for strength.

The Fair Is Here

Here comes the parade, with flags and bands and floats and fire engines; youngsters on decorated bicycles, Cub Scouts trudging manfully; the cavalcade, some riders proud, some casual. It's the day of the Guilford Fair.

On the grounds, the flurry of preparation settles into the timeworn pattern of the show.

Horses canter around the ring with riders trying to look at once nonchalant and professional, and the judge in the center taking notes. Now a jumper clips the top bar, knocking it off as an "O-o-o-oh!" of disappointment wells up in the crowd.

Draft horses lean into their collars to budge the loaded stone boat in the drawing ring, while the announcer keeps the boys in the bleachers hep with buddy-buddy country sportscasting.

Oxen stand for hours, epitome of patience, swishing tails at pesky flies, rocking widespread horns, chewing cud, awaiting the word that sends them into the ring.

Pigs lie in the straw, oblivious to flies, giving an occasional sleepy grunt.

Sheep are lined up in the show ring, young owners prodding them to stand squarely, judge feeling the wool and the hide, then standing back to think.

Heifers being groomed by 4-H Club members. Other future farmers sit on a bale of hay at the center of the tent, comparing their experiences and hopes.

In the needlework tent, women admire the work that's on display, and second-guess the judges' rating of the exhibits.

Fruit glistens behind the chicken wire stapled there to ward off predatory fingers. Sunflower stalks reach to the peak of the vegetable tent. Insurance Man Donald Adams and Lumber Man Edwin Bartlett are locked in annual competition for the biggest pumpkin.

Tomato juice? Yes, for years an unofficial trophy for the best tomato juice has shunted back and forth between Democrat Henry Graver and Republican Stanley Page.

In the food tent, too, are handsome cakes with little slices cut out where the judges — lucky people! — have sampled.

On the midway you can toss rings or coins or baseballs, or shoot pellets — endless ways to part with your money with maximum frustration and minimum return.

Children scream in wild excitement on the fast rides, or circle placidly on the merry-go-round. They gaze wide-eyed at animals they've never seen before, or reach between the slats to feel the soft wool on little lambs. They get into chocolate ice cream up to the ears. They demand the doll in the top row that only a miracle on the wheel of chance could get for them. They gloat over the blue ribbons on their vegetable entries. They tug restlessly at the hands of mothers who are talking with friends they haven't seen for years. They need to go to the bathroom. They are paged over the PA system when it's time to go home. Their mothers are paged when the kids get lost. But everyone is having fun. The fair is here.

Life and the Shelves

I'm sitting on the kitchen floor facing three empty shelves. Beside me is a huge basket full of canned goods. They were taken out of the cupboard so it could be painted. Now I'm trying to put them back in some semblance of system, so that when we want corned beef hash or cream of tomato soup we can find it, or at least know whether or not we have any.

But that's life. It's not easy to arrange your affairs so as to know what's available, and to reach it handily.

Here's soup. I'll start at the right hand side of the top shelf with that, and put entrees like salmon and hash at the left side, along with spaghetti and meat balls. Suddenly I notice that this shelf is the hardest to see for anyone who doesn't happen to be sitting on the floor. Yet I'm loading it with things we most often use. Better they should go where it's easier to see 'em. I'll take them all out and put them on the next shelf.

That's life. You may start on the wrong track. With luck you can switch before it's too late. Two years out of college, successful in graduate courses in education, I found that classroom teaching was not for me. Finally I found the shelf where I belonged — newspaper editor.

Right now I'm moving cans of soup from one shelf to another. Four cream of asparagus, six beef consomme. Must have been on sale. Chicken gumbo, cheddar cheese, split pea, but no cream of tomato.

That's life, also. Too much of one thing and not any of another. Taking what's marked down may be astute, but don't carry it too far. Slipshod planning leads also to "not enough."

Now here's ready-to-spread lemon frosting. I wonder if it's still good. That can was here last time we painted the kitchen. Why keep it?

Again, that's life. We cling to prejudices and procedures that don't fill any particular need, but get in the way of skills that are needed every day.

Down to the bottom shelf. The floor. The space is higher. That tall bottle of apple juice and the white vinegar will fit. Well, they would if I hadn't filled the space with smaller jars and cans. Once more I shift things, putting short containers on closer-spaced shelves.

Just like life, letting pint-sized problems fall into areas of time and capacity needed for important matters. One of my uncles liked to get little items out of the way, clearing the deck for the main job. For him, this was right because details bothered him. Generally, though, such priorities do not work. The tall shelf when needed is often cluttered with squatty cans.

Finally I sit back to admire my handiwork, and there comes to mind another aspect of life — the perilous area of the unknown; the home of adventure and opportunity. Into this very same cupboard almost a half-century ago we were stowing away a basketful of canned goods. They had been given to us in a pantry shower. The cans gleamed puckishly at us, shiny with all their labels removed! Open one! It may hold halves of peaches in heavy syrup — or it could be sauerkraut. That's life!

Not Too Short to Save

That pesky ball of string fell off my desk and rolled across the floor, unwinding as it went. When I caught up with it and began to rewind, I found a knot every couple of feet. The whole ball was made up of short pieces tied together. It put me in mind of the classic paper bag from someone's attic, labeled ''Pieces of String Too Short to Save.''

So I made an inquiry. Those pieces of string, I was told, are indeed too short to save at the home town newspaper plant where my wife used to work. When bundles of papers for office use are cut open, some of the girls can't see all that husky string going to waste, so they stuff it into bags and take it home for use around the house.

Likewise in pre-silo years on our farm, when cornstalks were bundled and stacked at the barn, the twine that held them was not thrown away when the bundles were cut. The short lengths were hung on a nail above the stalk cutter waiting to be used for emergency repairs to harness, or to tie up feed bags.

When I was a child I'd watch my grandmother cut old cloth into narrow strips, all colors in random order. She'd sew them together and roll the ribbon into an ever-growing ball. When enough was done, it was sent to a shop equipped to weave rag carpets, and that's what was on Grandma's floors.

Back to the ball of string on the desk. I was tired and edgy that day. Unstrung, you might say. Everything seemed to come in pieces too small to save.

''The web of our life is of a mingled yarn, good and ill together,'' says one of the Lords in Shakespeare's *All's Well that Ends Well*. He goes on to join the pieces: ''Our virtues would be proud if our faults whipped them not; and our crimes would despair, if they were not cherished by our virtue.''

It takes good tight knots to pull the whole thing together. Just mulling it over won't do. Think of this chap in Hillaire Belloc's *Cautionary Tales*: ''The chief defect of Henry King was chewing little bits of string.''

Or getting into a lighter vein with Henry Sambrooke Leigh: ''My love she is a kitten, and my heart's a ball of string.''

Today, time is short and string is long. When there was less string you needed to save it, even if it took time. Now if the girls figured their time at home the way they expect it to be calculated at the office, they'd find tying two-foot lengths of string together more costly than even the exorbitant price of a new ball of string.

Yet a vestige of the olden days lives in those girls who hate to throw away something that might be useful. They have the Yankee urge to save.

Plus the knack of tying square knots.

No Hidin' Place . . .

No stir of air, no rustle of leaves. Nature wraps the night in stillness. Yet its quiet cannot absorb the relentless roar that invades my bedroom — the oppressive sound of traffic on the Connecticut Turnpike a quarter-mile away.

Crescendos come as diesel trucks pound into the long level stretch after descending the hill, or as one of the monsters bites into the up-grade.

Noise has become part of the environment — a pollution as revolting as the foulness tainting some streams or insidious gases permeating the atmosphere. To me it is fatigue-producing, a substantial and obnoxious detriment to health.

Much of it is unnecessary. I cite the piercing racket of most motorcycles, wiping out all aural communication. In contrast to these I place John Hubbard, who drew as much pleasure from a motorcycle as anyone I ever knew, yet his fine-tuned machine spoke in a whisper — not a roar.

So much for the internal combustion engine as disturber of the peace, with a nod to its application in garden tractors and lawn mowers among which my own join in the suburban clatter.

Indoors I rank the vacuum cleaner's whine as one of the most annoying sounds in the universe. That and other household gadgets such as blenders and washing machines, however, have specific purposes with noise-making only an incidental side-effect. What about all the devices whose primary purpose is to create sound?

America is afraid of silence. Busyness and tension preclude quiet contemplation, or perhaps generate conditions too disturbing to contemplate. Hence the radio is on from dawn to bedtime whether or not anyone is paying attention to it. Music or an unreasonable facsimile thereof follows us through the supermarket or the lunch room. It can be a pleasant background, but more often it is imposed on all the other noises making easy conversation impossible.

Finally comes the ultimate insult. I place a telephone call and they put me on "hold" with canned music, hoping, I presume to appear hospitable while Mr. Gottrox concludes his conversation on another line and finds time for me. The illusion I get, however, is that the office force has gone off to coffee break leaving me behind a frustrating wall of music. I'm tempted to hang up.

See how crotchety the world's racket makes me? There's no relief. As I write this, the turnpike roars on, a high-decibel diesel pounds past the house, and a low flying plane lays down a barrage of dissonance!

Paging Johnny Chuck

Reading magazines is fun, but I wish the publishers would make it easier. They put too many road blocks in the way.

Let's say I spot a periodical on the newsstand with the lead story title in big bold type on the cover: "Woodchuck Loves Yogurt." That stops me. Why would anyone, human or otherwise, want to eat yogurt? How would a woodchuck come to have that hang-up? Does he scuttle up to the back door and wait for it? What's his favorite flavor? Will it make him too thin to hibernate? Can he keep his Candelmas date? Better find out about this.

To catch that title, incidentally, I had to by-pass the cover picture of a buxom gal in a biniki leaning forward to offer a carton of yogurt to a goggle-eyed groundhog. This brings to mind one of my lesser ambitions — to frustrate some unfortunate designer of book jackets by writing a best-selling novel whose leading lady is flat-chested.

Getting back to the magazine, I scan all the large print and fine print on the cover and finally find the price. A dollar and a half. Is it worth it? Probably not, but I have to find out about that woodchuck. I take the magazine to the counter and pay for it, plus tax.

Home in the easy chair, the first thing is to make the publication readable. Rip out those pesky reply cards that are tipped in every here and there.

Now I turn to the index. And turn. And turn. And turn. I go past about twenty full-page ads, through the letters to the editor, past the Statement of Ownership and the list of editorial and business staff, and then back again, to find the table of contents. There it is: "The Woodchuck Who Loves Yogurt . . . Page 53."

Here's the page. Is this the story? Oh, sure! The title is stashed away in the text, halfway down the page. It might even have been built into the full-page illustration on the facing page.

So I begin to read about the friendly marmot and his unusual diet. After a couple of pages I'm tripped up by the order, "Turn to Page 129."

Oh. It's a numbers game! The center 48 pages are on dull paper with a numbering sequence all their own. They're too elite to mingle with the hoi-polloi of columns dealing with yogurt and woodchucks and the like. Let's see. Does 129 come before that section or after it?

Two-thirds of the pages carry no number. The ads reach into the margins. Here's 87, so 129 has to be farther along. Now I see 145. Back to 123. I've got it surrounded! Flip ahead three sheets and there it is. No number, but here's a small heading, "Chuck Diet (From p. 56)." I keep a finger there and turn back to pick up the continuity. The search was distracting.

Oh, yes. Chucky got his yen for yogurt when the children left half a carton in the garden where he had been devouring succulent peas. I chase his tale through the ads, top of one page, bottom of the next, left, right, even center.

Nevertheless this has the edge over television, for I can skip the ads if they don't interest me. With TV I have to sit there wasting time while they try to sell me diapers. Often I wouldn't wait, not even to watch a woodchuck eat yogurt.

I Tend to Breathe

Dear Ann Landers:

I'm really worried about myself. I seem to be just a great big vacuum — a glob of nothingness waiting for something to fill it. Wherever I sit or stand, whichever way the wind blows, wherever the fan is pointed, it makes no difference. All the cigarette smoke drifts toward me, and stays there.

Once I was in a restaurant with my wife and some friends. We had just started in on some fresh salmon with wine sauce when a fellow and a girl at the next table lit their cigarettes. Soon we were gasping. What should we have done? Complain to the waitress? Ask the people not to smoke? Move to another table? We ate smoked salmon.

Yesterday I was chatting with a chap who had a lighted cigarette in his hand. He kept waving it in front of my face as he gesticulated. I backed away, but he moved right along with me until I was against the wall. How could I handle that situation without having the fellow get incensed?

I used to work in an office where my desk was between two others occupied by chain smokers. One of them often left a butt in the ash tray, giving off more smoke than when she was puffing on it. I was inhaling more than she was. What should one do in such a case? Put a note in the suggestion box? Leave an anonymous letter on the desk? Snitch all their matches? Get a different job?

Don't tell me to call a meeting, please! No way in the world can you get your eyes and lungs so full of smoke as by sitting in a conference room where the puffs get deeper and deeper as the tension builds up. Lighters click frantically in trembling fingers, butts pile up in ash trays, the air is blue. No, a meeting wouldn't help at all.

You know, Ann, I was thinking the other night about the Indians who are now in the Happy Hunting Grounds. Maybe you believe in eternal life and maybe you don't, but anyway, I was wondering if they look down on Manhattan Island which they sold cheap, and on all the green land that was taken away from them, and chuckle when they see how the tobacco they introduced to the settlers is killing palefaces faster than they could ever have hoped to do with their tomahawks and muzzle-loaders.

Isn't it silly for the government to put part of our hard-earned tax money into subsidies for tobacco growers, and at the same time use more of it to tell the public that smoking is dangerous?

A fellow claims a constitutional right to smoke whenever and wherever he wants to. How about my constitutional right to some clean fresh air? I really do have a strong tendency to breathe, Ann. Is that unreasonable?

Seen On The Green

Guilford Green lies cool and quiet in morning sunlight. My early-opening eyes love the beauty which they see, the recollection of things seen at other times, the contemplation on what was seen by other eyes long closed. Vision brings the tableaux, one by one:

This bench, where lovers caress and kiss, oblivious to all else; that one where a loner delves into some philosopher's paragraphs; and yonder another where two old men review their common memories.

Memorial tablets on boulders, and statue honoring those who have served and died. Flags are unfurled, marching feet respond to drum beat; aching hearts to bugle call.

Blankets on the grass and chairs unfolded as folks relax to hear a concert under the stars of a summer night.

Paintings hung on lines, handcrafts in tents where all may come to look, admire, perhaps buy.

Rides, calliope, games, lights as firemen raise funds for their service to the town.

Strawberry, peach — whatever shortcake festival. Tables loaded with plants or pies for sale.

Oxen waiting patiently to draw a load; herdsmen grooming livestock; benches bearing pullets, pumpkins, pickles, quilts; merry-go-round and ferris wheel; it's the Guilford Fair!

Soft silent snow reflecting gleams of light from lone white candles of Christmastide in church and home.

Elm trees a hundred strong and a century old, laid low by hurricane, their great roots wrenched from rain-soaked soil lifting sections of cement walks aloft.

Square bandstand, green-painted waiting through rain and sun for concert day.

Auctioneer sweating to draw best bid for hay to be harvested from the Green.

Quill pen scratching out a contract as four citizens sign to care for Green and fence in return for hay crop.

Women in sunbonnets, aprons, long skirts, the United Workers for Public Improvement, raking leaves and discussing funds for street lights.

Setting posts and fastening rails for a fence around the Green in 1837.

Elm saplings, set ten years earlier, reaching for the sky.

Oxen drawing off stone boats laden with gravestones, as the living Green supercedes the churchyard burying ground.

Congregational Church, Episcopal Church, Town House, four school houses, hay scales all grace the Green.

Posted notice: "No more trees shall be cut downe upon the Greene before the meeting house."

Ox carts turned away by law forbidding gravel removal.

Water in pond holes shimmering in the breeze as stage coaches rumble along Boston Post Road, kitty-corner through the Green. Grazing cattle raise their heads to watch.

Pacing, sighting, measuring, mapping — Guilford's founders reserve a common Green.

One Chance in 7,178,667

What are the odds? About three to one, I'd say, that the numbers on the dial when I spin the pointer on my post office box will open the door on an offer — sweepstakes numbers already registered in my name, giving me a chance to win $50,000.

Something like that arrives several times a week. Occasionally the words "Pay to the order of . . ." show enticingly through the address opening in the window envelope. I rip it open and there indeed is a check for $50,000.00, made out to Mr. H. P. Dudley, but with NOT NEGOTIABLE stamped across its face. With it is a four-page letter in which the warm and friendly computer has called me by name every two or three paragraphs. What could be more beguiling?

Books, magazines, records — whatever the mailing is peddling — are described in detail, telling all the advantages they might bring me. Furthermore, I don't have to pay now. The $36.00 will be billed in four monthly installments with no finance charge, no annual percentage rate of interest. Still, it would take three more 20-cent postage stamps than a single payment would. I program that into my pocket computer which instantly tells me that it would equal an interest rate of about thirteen per cent per annum on the unpaid balance.

According to some fine print on the back of the flier, the approximate numerical odds of winning the grand prize are one in 21,536,000. Since my certificate carries three numbers, let's say my chances are increased to one in only 7,178,667. Even so, since I don't want to buy anything, putting $36.00 on the line in hopes of winning $50,000 is a gamble I doubt Jimmy the Greek would recommend. Even a 20-cent stamp on the NO envelope would be a poor investment at those odds.

Considering that postage stamp again, I wonder just who would take a licking? Returning 7,178,667 certificates would take $1,435,733 in postage. The folder flourishes $325,000 as the total of all prizes. To implement the distribution of less than a third of a million dollars the postal system would garner almost a million-and-a-half dollars of business, paid for by more than seven million losers.

This calculation of course by-passes variables and related factors. For example, the post office had to handle a vast number of the original announcements which traveled at the low rates of bulk mail. Nor have I programmed in the statistical impact, if any, of the lesser prizes offered in the same sweepstakes. The odds, though, are too overwhelming to be wiped out by such considerations.

"If you don't want to enjoy these superb books, return your sweepstakes certificates in the NO envelope. You'll still be eligible to win a prize." That's what the law requires and that's what the folder says. I don't doubt it. Yet psychological coercion lurks there — a nagging uneasiness about all those NO envelopes shunted into one basket while the YES ones go another way so that the orders can be filled.

Incessant use of the sweepstakes ploy indicates that it produces sales. It feeds on the incorrigible optimism of humankind. Odds are distorted by never-ending hope, and hidden risks are not recognized. In the average mind the balance is tilted toward winning the raffle, and against the likelihood that the meter maid will come along to tag the parked car.

Now what's this printing just above the perforated line? TEAR OFF AND MAIL. That does it! I resent being pressured. Even if I wanted to send the letter I would not go dashing out to the mail box with it. Odds bodkins!

High-Jacker

I'm full of get-up-and-go on a brisk October morning. The garage door opens and the sun streams in onto the car, but the vehicle is atilt. One tire is flat, right on the bottom where a tire can look flat.

Still, that doesn't deflate my spirits. I'll call Triple-A or my service man. No, I won't. Fifty years ago that thought wouldn't have entered my mind. Why should it now? I can shift that wheel in less time than it would take a service man to get here.

Everything's ideal. The jack can set square and firm on the cement floor. It's not soft ground where the base of the jack sinks out of sight. It's not a hummock so high the jack can't be fitted underneath the car. It's not in a downpour of rain, nor in the dark. It's not in traffic where shifting a tire is inviting the undertaker. I can get into old clothes and not mess up a good suit. Sink and soap are handy for clean-up when the job is done. Do it yourself, Dudley!

Besides, I've had this car three years and not yet carried out a drill in wheel changing. It's time to see just how everything works. Out comes the instruction manual. Down comes the rack that holds the spare tire underneath the trunk. The jack is tucked away in a hidden nest under the hood. It looks like a good one, but needs a squirt of oil to make the screw turn easier.

I have a long-standing relationship with jacks — countless ups and downs. First was for wagon wheels, a wooden device with little steps notched into its business end to fit various heights. Fit it under the axle of the buggy, push down the long handle, and up came the wheel. Yes, the tire was flat, but it was forged that way, of iron. This was a lube job, loosening the nut, slipping the wheel off, smearing grease on the axle, putting the wheel back and letting the jack down.

Then came the Model T Ford. Its simple straight-up screw jack was actuated by a ratcheted handle. Set it under one of "Tin Lizzie's" honest axles and lift the wheel without any problem. My first Chevy was almost like that, too, but I went for the luxury of a hydraulic jack from Sears Roebuck.

All too soon automobiles outgrew their wheel-bases. Sleek hoods and long trunks and fancy bumpers got in the way. Fenders curved over the wheels. The jack had to have a long handle. Juggling it into place was a neat trick, especially in a rough roadside spot.

Still later came the loose-jointed monster cars that had to be lifted sky-high before a dangling wheel would clear the ground. They brought the bumper jack, one of the most lethal booby traps ever devised. Change the tire if you dare, but don't get near the tilted-up car while doing it!

My entrance into the tire-changing world coincided with the advent of the demountable rim. I had to learn that the lug bolts on the left side of the car had left-handed threads. On the old buggy there was good reason for threading the axles that way, so the rotation of the wheel wouldn't tend to loosen the nut. On the rim of the automobile wheel, though, that seemed to me to be a vestigial anachronism.

To pry the tire off the rim with a pair of flat irons without pinching the inner tube was a fine art. The split rim of later years made it a little easier.

Remember the tube-patching kit? From the cardboard can, dump out a little tin grater, a tube of cement and a sheet of patch. Find the leak in the tube by dunking it into a tub of water and watching for the bubbles. Rough up the area, put on cement, peel the backing off a piece of patch, roll it on tight with the edge of the can. Find the nail puncturing the shoe, pull it out, work the tube into place, pump it up, and away we go!

Those days are gone. Tire mounting is merciless, tires are tubeless, the job is hopeless. Take it to a professional.

But I master the new Peugeot jack, change the tire, and am ready to go in 20 minutes. Next time, it'll take only ten.

Why? Because!

Exasperating, insistent and oftentimes productive is the three-letter question, "Why?" At least it looks like a three-letter word, even though the alternative

pronunciation "wy" makes it lose a letter; and the question mark that follows it is almost a fourth one.

Daily it reflects picayune irritations. Why does salad dressing come in bottles shaped so there's no possibility of getting the last of the contents out? Why can't I buy just one high-intensity bulb instead of having to take a package of two? Why can't I find my sweater? Why didn't that guy signal for his left turn?

Not at all superficial, though, is the child's incessant "Why?" It's the foundation of learning. Why does the sun come up? Why do you put flour in the cake? Why does Margaret have to go to school? Why can't I play in the street? Why does the fly keep buzzing against the window? Why does the newspaper have black letters?

Having asked a question, the youngster is likely to remember the answer, so it ought to be clear and accurate. Not always does it come out that way. I remember that my patient father would sometimes respond simply, "Because."

Often I accepted that. I guess I sensed the why of "because." Probably my father was tired, or was thinking about something more important. Perhaps the question was so deep that even he couldn't explain it. Or maybe he thought the answer would be too much for me to understand.

At another level we find that the path of progress is the pursuit of "Why?" A classic example is Newton's speculation about why the apple fell on his head rather than sailing off into space. The scientist, the physician, the philosopher, the economist, the politician, all find motivation in "Why?"

But "Why" can be devastating.

Take the day I kicked the lunch box. It was after-school and one of the boys had set his lunch box on the ground while he went back into the building for something. I came running around the corner, saw this box in the path and without breaking stride gave it a swift kick.

The box, made of cardboard-like composition — a predecessor of plastic — sailed through the air, crashed and was practically obliterated. Just then the owner came out, and quite predictably indicated a strong inclination to obliterate me.

"Why did you do that?"

All right, why? Did I want to pick a fight? Did I hold a grudge against this schoolmate? Had he done anything to make me seek revenge? Was I trying to teach him not to leave his belongings around so care-lessly? Was I destructive by nature? Did I want to show everyone how far I could kick a lunch box? Was I testing the toughness of the box? Was someone egging me on? Did I think about neatening the school yard?

No, not any of those. I could not find an answer. Logically I offered to buy him a new lunch box, but he didn't want that. He wanted me to give him a reason, and I couldn't satisfy that insistent demand. There was no ''why'' for that impulsive kick — almost a reflex action.

A psychiatrist might have found some latent quirk that would produce that act, if I had told him that my step-mother loved me dearly, that my father was a mail carrier, that I never owned a dog, that I liked my grandmother's ginger cookies, and other facts and foibles of my childhood. That self-knowledge might have changed my whole life. But I didn't seek help, for I was not worrying myself into depression over the incident.

On the other hand, I was not proud of it. Neither then nor in the ensuing sixty years have I put it entirely out of my mind.

Why? Because!

No Hurry

Our neighbor Edward E. Griswold was a sagacious farmer not easily stampeded into precipitate action. Walking home from his tomato field after a day's work, hoe over shoulder, he paused at my grandfather's barn for a chat. Then, as he started to move along, my grandfather said, ''Don't be in a hurry, Ned.''

''Nope. Nope. I'll go before I get in a hurry.''

Suspicious Car

I suspect that I once had a suspicious car. I read about them in the police blotter, and wonder how a vehicle can be suspicious. The more I mull it over, the more it seems possible. Yes, I may have owned one!

This was a sedate sedan of 1928 vintage, dark green with black disc wheels. Part of her modesty was a little roller shade that could be drawn inside her rear window. Her background was impeccable. I named her Minnie, after the gray-haired lady who previously owned her and doubtless never drove more than 30 miles an hour.

Minnie was tough and dependable. She responded readily to the demands that this youngster, fresh out of college, placed upon her. Still, I have a haunting fear that she was suspicious.

One night I took my girl friend for a rural ride. Old-timers had told me that West Pond Road originally came out on the East-West Turnpike. We set out to see if that were true. After two or three miles the dirt road narrowed. Encroaching underbrush scraped Minnie's sides. I had to take care that she didn't straddle rocks that might crack her oil pan. I even had to keep both hands on the steering wheel. Finally we did emerge at the East-West Pike.

Next evening the Guilford Town Players sprung a picnic for the stock company staging shows at the Chapel Playhouse. Clearly it was my duty to see that no actress lacked a ride to the outing. I let Minnie drift tentatively past the Playhouse when the show was about to let out. Suddenly I sensed that the drifting was even less than tentative. Minnie was not about to go anywhere at all!

Why, after accepting the rough trek the night before, did she choose this crucial moment to show the chronic weakness of her ilk — a broken rear axle, on perfectly smooth pavement at three miles an hour? Did modest Minnie question my motives? Was she distrustful? Suspicious?

"Suspicious," however, may mean "tending to excite or cause suspicion." That's probably what the pedantic police blotter reflects. In this sense, I confess, I did make Minnie a suspicious car. At the time, I was a milkman, and made weekly mid-day trips to collect from customers who wanted to pay regularly and to give special attention to the few who didn't want to pay at all. The latter might not answer the doorbell if they spotted the delivery truck, so I would fox them occasionally by using Minnie. Predictably, she soon became as "suspicious" as the truck.

Yet the "inclined to suspect" definition seems to fit. With built-in idiosyncrasies and taken-for-granted reliability, Minnie was almost human. Inevitably, senility set in. A little crack opened in her head, letting water from the cooling system into one of her cylinders so that she limped along on five instead of purring at the usual smooth gait of six.

I never told her that rehabilitation would not be economical. But did she notice that I was taking the flashlight out of the glove compartment and the old work jacket from the trunk? Did she sense my sadness at the prospect of parting with a faithful friend?

We headed for the Madison Garage where a brand new Chevy awaited me. All at once the missing cylinder began to fire. The engine came to velvety smoothness. On the straightaway we burst into a glorious, illegal final fling at 75 miles an hour! Why did Minnie rally? Was she telling me something? Did she fear I would abandon her? Was she a suspicious car? I'm suspicious!

Looking for What I Find

Sunlight warms the soft gray of the spider web curving in graceful contour across the corner of the attic window sash. Such beauty built into a utilitarian structure is rarely equalled by human talent. Pity that the architect and builder and manager who lurked in the deep dark vortex of this web during the hot summer days is gone.

On the window sill flashes the iridescent body of a blue-bottle fly — a jewel set into that narrow band of

debris. He managed to avoid the silken trap, yet succumbed to the inevitable when old age silenced his day-long buzzing attacks on the unyielding window pane.

The sunbeam wants to dazzle me. It's playing on the antique mirror that leans against the washstand, only an arms-length away. But it is frustrated, dimmed by the blanket of dust that clings to the silver-backed glass. Reflected there is not the piercing sunbeam, but rather an aura of repose concomitant with years of retirement — rest from a century of helping people fuss over their hair and straighten their ties.

That's a deep blue window curtain hanging over the edge of the washstand — tossed aside impatiently by someone delving into the old trunk to find some special item, or perhaps laid there casually with the intent of folding it into a snug square pad and stowing it away some day. But now it hangs in graceful folds, draped with stunning effect by the unpredictable hand of chance.

See how that old chair stands out from the wall at an angle that seems to say, "Come; sit here and rest and think." Its air of genial invitation is in contrast to the stiff stance of its companion pieces, lined up against the wall straight-backed and grim, as if awaiting who knows what firing squad.

Three shelves of the bookcase carry their loads all straight and neat, but on the upper one two volumes inch forward from the line and a half-dozen draw back in disarray. Across them lies one more — a horizontal invitation for head-tipping to see what its title may be. On the bottom shelf the yellowing newspaper's bold headline proclaims PEACE and I look to see whether it be of 1945 or 1918, or perhaps even 1864.

Straight through the long middle "aisle" of the garret stretch the floor boards and the cracks between them. They point, they lead, they almost entice me toward the window in the far gable. Yet their hypnotic monotony is shattered by that rolled-up rug lying kitty-corner across the path, just beyond the chimney. Without it, one might envision bowling pins set at the end of the alley; with it, the illusion is lost.

To one side stands a dull red-painted chest in stark severity; but hanging over its top edge is the tip of a red ski cap, breaking the sharp topline of the massive piece. Just as its softness so often warded off the relentless bite of winter wind, so now it relieves the harsh visual edge of the furniture. A sensitive photographer might make a prize-winning picture, catching it at just the right angle.

The little red fire engine with a front wheel missing noses out from its niche in the toy pile. The bell is on the hood, and the driver at the wheel. Just as it's about to roll, the years roll back instead. I hear not the siren, but instead a sharp admonition from sixty-five years ago: "Don't leave that there. Somebody will trip over it."

Very well. We can make the attic neat. It can be put in order, its personality changed. Then we can find what we're looking for. But I reap a very special reward by going to the attic simply looking for what I find.

Baffled by the Bag

"Why change bags?"

"Because I can't carry a blue handbag with this brown coat."

"Better get a black bag. That'll go with anything."

"I can't take a black bag in the summer, and besides, they aren't wearing black this season."

Such is the ritual of departure. Often it includes shifting things from one bag to another. Which items have to go this time? The clutter and decisions take even longer if the change happens to be from the full-fledged handbag to the tiny evening purse. The minutes tick away as I stand there sweating in my overcoat and twirling my keys.

Consider a partial inventory of the contents of the typical handbag. Never mind any particular order. Take it the way things fall out when dumped on the table:

Wallet with folding money, charge cards and photos of grandchildren; plastic rain hat; comb; hair net; cough drops; newspaper clipping; compact; grocery coupons; keys; tissues; shopping list; flashlight; toothpicks; letters to mail; nail file; check book; chewing gum; three part-rolls of Certs; date book; breath freshener; earrings; theater program; postage stamps; three pencils; handkerchief; pen.

The list could go on and on, with variations according to the needs and whims of the owner, and the time span since the last hoeing out.

The presence and use of the handbag in the home are matters to be conjured with. When she says, "Would you bring me my pen, please? It's in my handbag right there on the hall table," I don't try to pick out the pen. I'd never find it. The handbag has three sections, one with zipper, each stuffed with paraphernalia. I don't pour the stuff out onto the table; I could never fit it all back in. I just bring the bag to her so she can fish out the pen.

So much for the home. Now slip on your topcoat and go out into the world with me, where the handbag reigns. Stand in line at the grocery check-out counter, the post office window or the bank teller's cage, and watch.

Here's a lady delving into her bag, pawing like a puppy trying to unearth a bone. She's grappling for two pennies, thinking she can find them quicker than the clerk could flip three from the cash register. Another is looking for her pen to write a check, or fumbling for the grocery list to be sure she has picked up everything she needs.

Then whatever came out has to go in again, plus a pack of cigarettes, with some rearranging. It's fascinating to watch, unless you happen to be behind four other people in the line, and in a hurry.

Handbag design is a problem for an engineer — probably a woman engineer — not a fashion designer. It's not to be taken lightly. In fact, it has become so heavy that a shoulder strap is often added. I once saw an over-designed bag with so many pockets and sections that it was loaded with the weight of its own leather. It was for a super-orderly person with a strong back.

Tight snaps and double handles may discourage the purse-snatcher — but why carry a lot of money? I suspect that winnowing through the contents of most handbags would be about as profitable as panning for gold in a Guilford creek.

So much for the handbag. The woman lives by it; the boyfriend wonders at it; the husband is baffled by it. I'm not going to delve into it any more.

Birds of a Feather

It's October. The sun breaks over the eastern horizon more and more toward the south each morning. The air is cool with a friendly briskness. The grass is tipped with white frost that lingers in the shade of the pine tree and the house, but vanishes with the touch of sunshine.

Along the stone wall a squirrel scampers, lugging a big black walnut. The leaves are falling, but this morning three of the great maples are laden with life — solid with blackbirds that have swarmed there like bees.

Call it a flock, though — not a swarm — and listen. Was there ever more relentless chatter? A more impenetrable wall of sound? Well, yes, I've heard almost the same thing by standing aside for an objective moment or two at a lively cocktail party. Those birds are talking en masse. They're almost like people. Perhaps some are listening, but that's not evident.

I see other analogies between fall-flocking blackbirds and the habits and foibles of mankind. Three or four just flew past the window as I sit here at the typewriter. Then two more. Nothing for a little while, then twos and threes and sixes, all headed in one direction. Just the same way, on the road beyond, people are passing — a couple of cars, a gap, two more, gliding off to join the busy crowd.

Now the whole flock descends like a swirling, wind-blown cloud and settles on the lawn and in the field beyond — a blanket of blackbirds. I use the term "blackbird" in the dictionary sense, not the ornithological. Many of the aggregation are handsome, iridescent purple grackles. With them are starlings and cowbirds, and probably red-winged blackbirds in somber winter attire. That's human, too — the congregation of compatible but different people in a common cause.

Even with all that togetherness, though, each bird is walking and looking and grabbing for himself. The aim is to get some seeds to eat, and that's an individual matter. What could be more like us?

I notice that the blanket has moved a little way

across the open field. The flock didn't fly, nor are all the birds walking in any one direction. Now I see how it's done. A few from the rear ranks fly up and leap-frog to the front. Now isn't that progress in human terms? Individuals who feel under-privileged; those who are aggressive; those with special talent — all such catapult themselves over the apathetic mass. That's how new fields are opened up in science, industry, politics and culture.

Suddenly the whole flock takes off in unison. In an incredible instant the land is clear. Was it danger? That's the way individual efforts are melded into disciplined action and selfishness turns to sacrifice when peril such as war threatens a human group. Or was it a false alarm? Did one or two panic and all the rest flee without bothering to find out why — just as people often do?

Now they are circling back and settling in on the very area they left. They've resumed the routine of walking, probing, chattering in guttural tones, leap-frogging in little groups, occasionally having little tiffs over extra rich morsels.

How should I interpret that? Are they like the people who persistently refuse to learn from experience or history; who go back to the flood plain and rebuild after the inundation; or restore an economic system whose built-in tensions have brought catastrophe? Or should we say that this reflects the courage of all the common folk, and the valor of the great ones, who have refused to be turned from their purposes and have achieved success against great odds?

Now the birds have drifted away. I stroll out there and my presence triggers the screaming alarm of the blue jay. First-fallen leaves rustle underfoot, and later ones are drifting down. It's autumn, full of beauty; the resumé of summer, the foreword of winter, the time for contemplation.

Katydids

Tonight the katydids are lulling me to sleep, even though they sound more excited than sometimes because it's a hot night in August. The katydid beats a faster tempo in warm weather than in cool. I believe there's a formula for determining the temperature from the speed of his beat.

The dictionary says: "*katydid* (ka-te-did), n., any of several large, usually green, American long-horned grasshoppers, the males of which produce a characteristic song. (imit.)"

The etymologist is obviously no entomolgist. That's not a song; it's an instrumental performance. The katydid doesn't use his vocal cords; he fiddles away with his hind leg. The result, however, is certainly characterisitic and it really does "(imit.)" — "Katy-did! She did! She didn't!"

Folklore has it that the sound of the first katydid in August foretells the first frost of autumn to be just six weeks away.

I like katydids because, along with crickets and tree toads, they are part of the chorus which, when I was very, very young, my father used to call "sleepy noises." It's also because they are harbingers of autumn, my favorite time of year.

I associate katydids, too, with the times we'd stay

at my grandmother's place in North Madison. It was quiet there at night — the kind of stillness you can find hardly anywhere any more. I could hear the brook tumbling over its stony bed in the hollow across the road. The whip-poor-wills whistled to each other on the hillsides beyond. And the katydids sawed away in soporific symphony.

The katydid is etched deep into my consciousness also in a totally different context. This was a September night. The air was crisp. The countryside lay in the light of a full moon. The fire alarm sounded,

and that was a call to action for this newshound. I talked my way through the police roadblock on the narrow lane leading to the Monastery. There, the fire was in an automobile driven straight up against the main doorway. Immolated in that car was a novice nun.

Turning from this macabre scene I drove slowly, very slowly back along the narrow road, wondering at the infinite mystery. Why would this act of violence be superimposed upon a setting of serenity beyond description?

The air was still, the moon rode gloriously high, and over it all sounded the fullest, richest katydid chorus I've ever heard. Both the violence and the tranquility were intensified in my consciousness by their simultaneous presence. That night I wrote:

''The tranquility of nature and the peace of perpetual prayer sustained a momentary shock, administered by someone who had failed to find peace of any kind in an unsettled topsy-turvy world.''

When The Milk Had Cream

The milk truck just went past. You might not recognize it as such. It looks more like the truck that delivers gasoline, but its huge tank is of gleaming stainless steel. It stops at the farm across the street, where milk is pumped into it from the cold holding-tank, and away it goes to the processing plant.

In the last seventy years I've seen vast change in the way milk comes from the barn on that same farm. There my grandfather milked his one or two cows, rhythmic streams strumming into the pail all warm and foamy. He carried it to the pantry in the house and poured most of it into shallow pans. Some went into a four-quart pail which was let down into the well in summer to keep cool. In the pans, cream rose and was skimmed off next day and put into an earthen jar eventually to be worked with a wooden paddle until butter and buttermilk separated.

Of my grandfathers's sons, only Paul stayed on the home farm to operate it. He found employment also in a crayon factory in the next town. Taking milk to one of the shop's employees each morning, he soon found other customers along the way. He added racks fore and aft on his bicycle to accommodate the bottles. He added to his herd of cows, and put up a small building equipped for cooling, bottling and storing milk.

When the crayon business lagged and the shop shut down during the summers, Paul Dudley developed a more extensive milk route focusing on summer residents at the shore. His Maxwell touring car was the delivery wagon. Then came more prosperous summers when the crayon shop kept working. Hence I became a milkman each summer during my college years, and year-round for several years more.

Finally Paul left the crayon shop and became a full-time farmer and dairyman — full-time to him meaning 4 a.m. to 9 p.m. seven days a week. A modern plant for pasteurizing and bottling, two delivery trucks, a second barn and a large herd of cows, with hay and ensilage production to support them, made Hill Crest Farm one of the most successful in the area.

From the rows of stanchioned cows in those barns to doorsteps all over Guilford and Madison, Hill Crest milk proceeded under care and control of a single, family-centered establishment. Here was an unbroken chain of responsibility the like of which is now rare. Anyone who wished could come and see the whole process.

Hill Crest milk had yellow cream at the top of the bottle — cream which if carefully poured off could be whipped; or if you shook the bottle you'd have milk of richness now no longer found. Few live today who know the joy of drinking cold milk that hasn't been marred by processing, adding or subtracting.

With keen competition in those free-enterprise times, milk distribution was appallingly inefficient. Delivery trucks of at least nine other dealers coursed through the streets of the area every day. Now all that is over. Milk has become a grocery item. People pick it up at the store, not at their doorsteps. Only one or two of the ten dealers survive.

Milk comes now in a paper carton, so you couldn't see the cream even if it were there. It's laced with vitamins and preservative, and homogenized. Such is the adaptation to our times and conditions. But I'd love to taste once again whipped cream such as my grandmother used to make from the skimming of those milk pans in her pantry!

A Season to Remember

It's a glorious celebration — this cascade of beauty descending upon the New England countryside. The trees and shrubs have done their summer stint. From the rising of sap and the burgeoning of buds in spring, they went on to put forth the foliage that purified our air and sheltered our activities.

Now, as they unfold a final proud display, can it not be said that they are relishing a sense of accomplishment?

In my college days, a little group falling into a midnight ''bull session'' might revert to the time-worn poser: If no ear were within hearing distance, would Niagara Falls be producing sound? The discussion would run into endless definitions and perceptions. My position , stubbornly maintained, was that the sound would be there whether or not it was detected.

Similarly, I envision the deep reds and clashing yellows of forest foliage shedding full brilliance even no eye may be within range. Carrying the concept another step, we may assume the spirit of celebration to be present whether or not any human interpreter be involved.

This postulate may be perceptive, or fanciful. No matter. October still seems to me the greatest month in which to be alive. Maples bring to climax the glory of the hillsides, while oaks fling a curtain of deeper tones and drop acorns for prudent squirrels to stash away. The Virginia Creeper flashes its red through the green sprays of cedar which it has invaded.

I see the crows foraging in the rustling cornstalks where bright yellow pumpkins hide. Brash blue jays scream warning of my approach. Crisp is the carpet of fallen leaves. Chickadees and a lone woodpecker scavenge for morsels under the loose bark of the old maple tree.

Autumn is for evaluation not merely of a year, but of a lifetime; for contemplating what has been; for appreciating all of it and mayhap memorializing some of it. I give you the words of Charles D. Hubbard, penned in the brilliant October of 1935 upon the untimely death of his good friend, my father:

''There is crimson and gold over the hillside; there is gold and crimson through the valley, and it sifts through the dark spruce tree to lie gloriously upon turf and pale marble. Yet all the beauty of the season seems but to reflect the splendor of a spirit which has walked among us.

"With what quiet, unassuming mastery were his labors accomplished! Many men fulfill obligations if convenient. Horace Dudley could at all times be counted upon. His sense of humor, balanced as it was by thoughtful consideration, made his companionship a delight. He gave thought for those whom he loved. He gave of his life for the world.

"As flutters to the ground an autumn leaf, so rests his form. But behind his kindly features, somewhere within was that which cannot be held captive in any grave nor be comprehended in any language.

"Now the crimson, it stands for sacrifice; and the gold, it stands for triumph. Death is swallowed up in victory, and down through the interminable vista of the future shall we feel the sweet, compelling admonition of a life triumphant."

Thus does autumn fall into harmony with human need for review and celebration. It is a setting for re-capitulation; an inspiring pattern for recognition of things well done; a foundation for re-grouping aims which have eluded consummation. It is a season to reap, review, relax, refresh, remember.

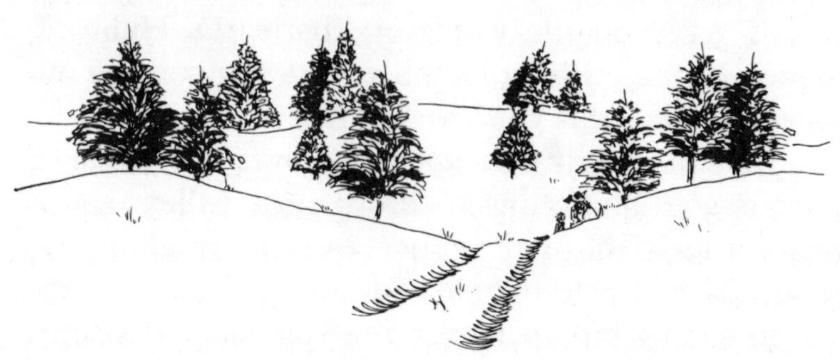

They

They say . . . They aren't wearing . . . They think . . . Yes, you hear "they" all the time. Who are they? Elusive, irresponsible infiltrators!

Recently I got my private eye, Cyclops Holmes, on the phone.

"Cyclops," I said, "I want you to find out who 'they' are."

"They? What do you mean, 'they'?"

"That's just what I mean. They. Whoever it is who led my wife to believe that there's a world-wide coffee shortage, when the supermarket shelves arc loaded with it."

"That'll take a month!"

"Maybe a lifetime. But the budget says two weeks. See what you can do."

Yesterday the phone rang. "This is Cyclops. I'm in Darien visiting my sister. I've solved the 'they' mystery. Outline is in the mail. I'll see you in a couple of days with the full report and my bill."

Here's Cyclops's four-point outline of the genealogy of "they":

1) Mary Murphy stops at Harry's Homeside Mart to pick up a pound of El Fragranco coffee. Harry is fresh out of that brand and she doesn't want any of the six others he has.

2) Helen Heathersworth breezes in for mid-morning coffee at Mary's place. "We'll have to use instant today," says Mary. "Harry doesn't have any El Fragranco."

3) At bridge that afternoon Helen says, "I wish it would rain. Nothing grows in this dry spell. Oh, your

coffee is heavenly, Marsha. Mary had to use instant this morning because Harry was out of El Fragranco."

4) At the club that night, the ever-lovin', full-fledged "they" emerges: "They say the drought in Brazil has created a coffee shortage."

Cyclops may have unearthed the definitive instance of conception, gestation and delivery of a domestic they.

Easier to trace is the commercial they. You look for an aqua dress, but can't find one anywhere. The clerks all say, "They aren't wearing aqua this summer."

No need to hire Cyclops on that one. They (the girls) are not wearing aqua because they (the designers and manufacturers) have put out nothing but beige this year. No normal woman would be seen in something they aren't wearing. It's a sure-fire gimmick to create programmed obsolescence and contrived demand.

World champion commercial they is the auto industry. Detroit thought they could sell steel and oil unlimited, until some of us turned to common-sense well-crafted smaller imports — so many of us, in fact, that we became an immaculately conceived counter — they. The Detroit they has to be bailed out. *Saturday Review* cartooned a classy Chrysler showroom with a sign, "Your Tax Dollars at Work."

Sometime I may ask Cyclops to find out why the domestic they tends to be the voice of doom. Take the weather, for instance. Whatever medium they use — television, radio, newspaper, almanac, or grandpa's sayings — they are dire and authoritative. "They say this hot spell will last three weeks more," or "They say we're in for the coldest winter in 40 years."

The doomsday they reaches its apex — or rather, nadir — in the fertile field of diagnostic and prescriptive medicine. They are far ahead of the profession, and less expensive, too. They recognize, interpret and even create symptoms. They don't have to worry about malpractice suits, because they can't be located. They know that sniffles come from fallout in Chinese A-bomb tests; that a paper bag over the head cures hiccoughs; that goose grease relieves chest congestion; that there's no help for cancer. They lurk and revel on the dark side.

Cyclops sagely noted, too, that whoever repeats anything they say automatically becomes part of the ever-growing they! When you do, you've been had!

Listening's All It Takes

A lesson in listening came on Election Day the year Guilford was divided into two voting districts. An irate citizen, frustrated by having come to the wrong polling place, charged into the office of First Selectman Leslie I. Dudley with a tirade on the folly of the two-district system. As abruptly as he had arrived, he turned and stalked out.

Les, who had not uttered a word during the outburst, took the cigar out of his mouth and with the trace of a grin, said, ''He feels better now!''

Touch of Thanksgiving

The touch of Thanksgiving used to be robust and intimate — as characteristic of the season as the irresistible aromas from Grandmother's kitchen.

Sunning in the southern lee of the woodshed is a pile of yellow pumpkins. Little globules of dew make their waxy skin more slippery than ever. Choose one to carry into the kitchen for a pie, but if you grab it by the stem, the touch of Thanksgiving is like cactus!

Great yellow ears of field corn crowd against the slats of the bins each side of the central aisle in the corn crib. The corn sheller stands in the middle. While I turn and feed the whirling, rasping contrivance, hold your hand under the cascade of kernels discharging into the half-bushel measure on the floor, and plunge it into the cool depth of the full measure.

In the field where the pumpkins and corn were harvested stand stacks of stripped stalks tied in bundles. As we cart them to the barn, this touch of Thanksgiving is harsh. The crisp leaves cut and irritate the skin. Stalks buckle and pinch the fingers. But we bring them in and shove them through the guillotine-like cutter so the cattle may find them more palatable.

Climb up to the hay mow. From the barn floor to the great beam, the post has been bored for pins that form a ladder, and those pins are worn glassy-smooth from the hands and feet that have traversed them during the years. Then, the tangled touch of fragrant hay is friendly, unless you happen to encounter the briers of a blackberry shoot that invaded the hayfield.

Now that you've tossed down some hay, distribute it along the cows' manger. Old Brindle extends her muzzle high to seek your touch, delicious scratching in the dusty-fuzzy feel under her long neck.

Hay from the salt meadows, brought in for bedding, has yet another texture, fine-stemmed and slippery, still with the smell of the sea.

Now to the feed room for hand-delving different than that in the corn house. Oats in a bin enticing your hand into the depths of smooth slim grains; a bag of bran, fluffy and clingy.

On the way back to the house, pick up the eggs. One lies in an open nest, cool and satiny. Another is under that setting hen. Welcome on the November day is the downy warmth you feel as you reach under her for the egg.

Going past the woodshed, take an armful along to the kitchen. The piles of split stove-length wood testify to the rugged touches of axe and saw. Each stick is ready, too, to leave a splinter in the unwary arm that lugs it to the house.

Grandmother's out of potatoes, so here we go to the cellar where their dry-earthy touch waits for us to gather them from the dark bin. Pimply little sprouts are just jutting from some of their eyes.

The kitchen is heavy with the aromas of turkey and turnip and onion and gravy. Uncles and aunts and cousins are arriving. The touch of hands in love and fellowship is here, with gratitude for hundreds of things we cannot lay our hands upon.

The touch of the old-time Thanksgiving Day — unlike the plastic bag, the cardboard box, the rock-hard package from the freezer of the 1980's — constantly reflected the labor the harvest had entailed, as well as the richness of life and the largesse of the land. It was tangible.

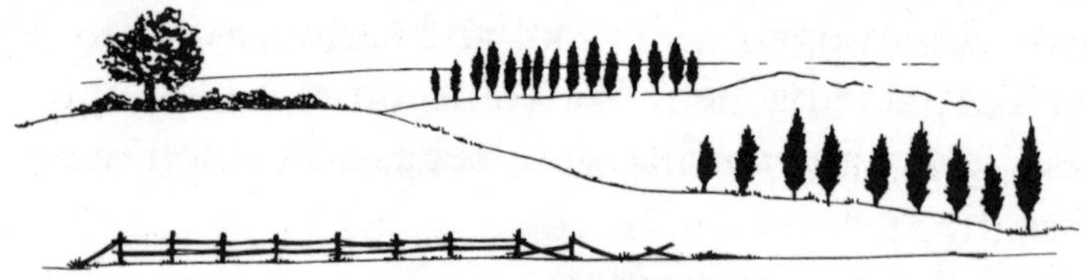

Big Game

The winter hunting season has just ended. Not to the fields and forests does this annual forage lead. It penetrates rather into the sky-tall timber of the city, and the dense thickets of tables and shelves and wall racks in quaint wayside ''shoppes.''

The aim is to bring down rare ''just-the-right-thing'' Christmas presents for relatives and friends. Usual weapons are small-bore wallets and double-barreled credit cards. I stagger home exhausted after tramping concrete lanes and vinyl-paved byways in the metropolis, and stumbling over four-inch changes of level in the tricky terrain of charming boutiques in rural settings.

Occasionally I count to see how many rounds of ammo for the wallet remain in my belt, and I calculate the prospects of reloading — or rather, recharging — the credit card.

Spectacular is this aspect of the great winter hunt. It's thrown at us in the newspapers and magazines, and on television day and night, picturing happy hunting grounds all over the map, abounding in big game and small.

Other challenges arise, though. I have done some poaching, bagging items for Christmas six months earlier while browsing in craft shops in Vermont or on Indian reservations in the West. I was trying to get ahead of the game, so to speak. Yet when winter comes, by golly I'm hunting again, delving through drawers and closets and attics and basements trying to remember where in heaven's name I stashed the summertime prizes. The excitement of the chase is on again!

Another seasonal hunt is for the Christmas tree. Of yore I would shoulder an axe or grab a hatchet, tramp out into our brush pasture, find a green and well-formed cedar tree, cut it down and proudly lug it home. No more. Now the weapon is the wallet, not the hatchet; the field, a commercial parking lot. The trees are cut and bound. The sport is like shooting fish in a barrel. Jounce the tree to see if the needles shed, pay the man, drape the tree over the car like a deer shot in Maine, and drive home with it.

Now I'm still hunting. The quarry is the stand I used to have to set the tree into. I scale the high reaches of the attic. If the quest succeeds, I also bring down boxes of lights and ornaments.

For food as well as sport the chase goes on. The protective coloration of a recipe card rivals that of a woodcock in November woods. Grandmother, of course, didn't need it. It was in her head — a lump of butter about the size of an egg, a pinch of salt, enough flour to make the dough feel right. But now it's printed in half-cups and teaspoons and ounces, and I need the card — so I hunt!

I comb another habitat — the bookcase — to ferret out a copy of "The Night Before Christmas . . ." I can't recite the whole poem. My grandchildren want to hear it. That hunt puts me also onto the trail of red stockings to hang by the fireplace. They may be in the cedar chest, but I don't count on it. The hunt is still a challenge.

I referred to the summer hunt as poaching, but that's unjust. There's never a closed season, although there may be a bag limit.

Now that it's all over, I look back on it. I followed many a trail, turned everything upside down, looked high and low, peered into every corner, traced innumerable scents, ran down each clue, spent ammunition in wallet and credit card. From some forays I staggered home loaded down; from others, empty-handed. In that frenzied diversity, I almost lost the biggest quarrry of all. Suddenly, there it was; I had corralled it — a happy Christmas.

No Cause for Worry

Among the staunchest of the faithful was Miss Fanny Dudley, who often walked two miles from her home to the church. As advancing age slowed her pace, neighbors made sure she had a ride. One was my cousin, Ralph Dudley, who drove a venerable Maxwell roughly equivalent to the "hot rod" of today's teen-ager.

"Doesn't it make you nervous to ride with Ralph?" inquired a solicitous friend.

"Why, no!" shot back Miss Fanny. "I figure he ain't a-goin' to carry me any faster'n he wants to ride himself."

The Mystery and the Glory

"Got your Christmas shopping done?"

Ten to one that's what your friend will ask when you meet him on the street this first week in December.

Yes, shopping seems to be what Christmas means to almost everyone. The carol has come to haunt the market place more persistently than it pervades the church. Christmas shopping is built into the people's psyche at this season.

The Santa Claus who used to be a single jolly elf swooping from the starry sky on Christmas Eve has now been cloned to "ho-ho-ho" simultaneously in dozens of stores and ring bells on many a frigid street corner.

My childhood Christmas centered around a cedar tree brought in from the pasture lot and decorated with pasted-paper chains, strings of popcorn and a touch of tinsel. Not Santa Claus, but my parents, grandparents and favorite uncle put the gifts on the tree after I'd gone to bed on Christmas Eve. The house had no fireplace with mantel from which stockings might hang.

For the last half-century my Christmas has been filled with the frustrations and the joys of making the music in our church reflect the mystery and the glory of the Advent and the Nativity.

It is from that mystery and that glory — the gift of a Savior to the Christian world, and the offerings of the Magi for the baby to whom their prophets and their star had directed them — that the giving of Christmas presents has evolved. This giving transcends mere "shopping." Love and thoughtfulness penetrate the wild wall of commerce.

Your friend doesn't mean merely, "Got your shopping done?" It's really, "Are your gifts all ready?"

Then you relax and think what Christmas means and why it came about. You re-live the Yuletide joys of all your life.

Christmas cheer is a lot of little things . . . Christmas tree lights reflected in the wide eyes of little boys and girls . . . Hanging stockings on the mantle in ecstasy of expectation . . . Young minds wrestling with the mystery of Santa Claus . . . Little foreheads and noses pressed against cold windows of the toy store . . . Family whisperings and clandestine stowing of parcels in closets and drawers . . . Chubby fingers untying gaily colored ribbons . . . Family ties renewed at holiday gatherings . . . The aroma of stuffed turkey . . . A pretty girl beneath the mistletoe . . . A candle in the window . . . Plum pudding . . . A card from the friend who never writes a letter . . . Carollers singing *Silent Night* . . . Stars twinkling far off in the clear cold night . . . The creak of dry snow underfoot . . . Laughter and the ringing of skates upon the ice . . . Reading the Christmas story . . . The happy greeting, "Merry Christmas!"